Alzheimer's and other forms of dementia are expected to triple in the next thirty years. While prevention and recovery strategies can help those afflicted at various stages, who cares for the caregivers? This book will help any caregiver navigate their new normal so that everyone involved in the caregiving process feels equipped, nurtured, and up for the task. Highly recommended.

DR. DANIEL G. AMEN, founder of the Amen Clinics for brain health, author of *Memory Rescue*

I must admit that I was reluctant to read *In the Lingering Light: Courage and Hope for the Alzheimer's Caregiver.* Why read a book I hope I never need? I am very thankful, though, that I overcame my hesitancy and met Cynthia Fantasia—and her husband, Bob—and accompanied her on her journey through this devastating disease. I was immediately drawn into her story and was challenged by her transparency and faith. While her insights and lessons are an indispensable resource for those who must walk this difficult path, her words encourage and equip the rest of us to support and care for those who are caregivers. Thank you, Cynthia, for your gift, not only to the Alzheimer's world but also to the body of Christ.

CYNTHIA HEALD, author of *Becoming a Woman of Excellence* and *The Faithful Way*

There's nothing easy abou
Alzheimer's disease, but C
that you can do more tha ain

JUL 2019

D1114047

you with grace and faith. Readers will find hope and encouragement within these pages.

JIM DALY, president of Focus on the Family

In the Lingering Light is a helpful read for anyone called to walk a difficult path. Cynthia Fantasia's tender and honest journey with God ministers grace and truth for life's most challenging times.

JEAN FLEMING, author of *Pursue the Intentional Life*

In the Lingering Light is one of those books everyone should have in their toolbox. At some point, we all will deal with Alzheimer's or one of the many forms of dementia that afflict our human frames. Having a wonderful guide who has walked the journey is a precious gift. Cynthia Fantasia is just such a guide. She's a naturally gifted communicator who speaks from personal experience and gently leads us through the process of saying good-bye to someone we love while they still live.

JAN SILVIOUS, author of *Courage for the Unknown Season*

CYNTHIA FANTASIA

IN THE
LINGERING LIGHT

Courage & Hope for the Alzheimer's Caregiver

A NavPress resource published in alliance
with Tyndale House Publishers, Inc.

NavPress is the publishing ministry of The Navigators, an international Christian organization and leader in personal spiritual development. NavPress is committed to helping people grow spiritually and enjoy lives of meaning and hope through personal and group resources that are biblically rooted, culturally relevant, and highly practical.

For more information, visit www.NavPress.com.

In the Lingering Light: Courage and Hope for the Alzheimer's Caregiver

Copyright © 2019 by Cynthia Fantasia. All rights reserved.

A NavPress resource published in alliance with Tyndale House Publishers, Inc.

NAVPRESS is registered trademark of NavPress, The Navigators, Colorado Springs, CO. The NavPress logo is a trademark of NavPress, The Navigators. *TYNDALE* is a registered trademark of Tyndale House Publishers, Inc. Absence of ® in connection with marks of NavPress or other parties does not indicate an absence of registration of those marks.

The Team:
Don Pape, Publisher
David Zimmerman, Acquisitions Editor
Elizabeth Schroll, Copy Editor
Julie Chen, Designer

Cover photograph of foggy road copyright © Stephanie Hulthen Photography/Lightstock.com. All rights reserved.

Author photo by Sharona Jacobs, copyright © 2018. All rights reserved.

All Scripture quotations, unless otherwise indicated, are taken from the Holy Bible, *New International Version,*® *NIV.*® Copyright © 1973, 1978, 1984, 2011 by Biblica, Inc.® Used by permission. All rights reserved worldwide. Scripture quotations marked NKJV are taken from the New King James Version,® copyright © 1982 by Thomas Nelson, Inc. Used by permission. All rights reserved. Scripture quotations marked NLT are taken from the *Holy Bible*, New Living Translation, copyright © 1996, 2004, 2015 by Tyndale House Foundation. Used by permission of Tyndale House Publishers, Inc., Carol Stream, Illinois 60188. All rights reserved.

Some of the anecdotal illustrations in this book are true to life and are included with the permission of the persons involved. All other illustrations are composites of real situations, and any resemblance to people living or dead is purely coincidental.

For information about special discounts for bulk purchases, please contact Tyndale House Publishers at csresponse@tyndale.com, or call 1-800-323-9400.

Cataloging-in-Publication Data is available.

ISBN 978-1-63146-911-4

Printed in the United States of America

25	24	23	22	21	20	19
7	6	5	4	3	2	1

This book is dedicated to my grandchildren:

Ryan, Nick, Avery, Tatum, and Natalie,

in whom Bob's legacy lives on.

CONTENTS

FOREWORD

I AM HONORED to introduce the author of this remarkable book. Cynthia Fantasia is my friend, and soon she will be yours, as you read this very personal disclosure of what happens when a marriage and a family are hit by the terrible blow called Alzheimer's.

Cynthia and I have been friends for more than forty years. Once upon a time, we raised our families in the same neighborhood. Within our church family, we participated in leadership of the women's ministry. I observed Cynthia steadily growing in all areas of leading others because she was so teachable herself.

I enjoyed watching (and applauding) as Cynthia became a speaker at women's events all over the United States. Her depth, honesty, vulnerability, and humor drew women in large numbers to hear her speak about what it means to be a follower of Jesus Christ.

Then, very suddenly, this wonderful ministry momentum was interrupted with the discovery that her husband, Bob, had been stricken with Alzheimer's. Cynthia had to deal with the question: *Will the things I've been talking about to women work in my own personal experience?*

The answer that followed? Absolutely!

Those of us who were in touch with Cynthia and Bob during those years were astonished at the faith, strength of character, and empathy that arose in Cynthia for her husband as he slowly declined into dementia. The simple truth is this: Cynthia loved her husband well.

In this book, Cynthia is painfully honest and, at the same time, very practical. She makes it possible for readers to learn how to live through the scourge of Alzheimer's with courage, stamina, and faith.

Throughout the book, Cynthia clearly reminds readers that Jesus' *lingering light* is always ready to break through the clouds in our lives. Readers will also pick up on the author's great concern for traps along the Alzheimer's journey, as the spouse becomes more and more the primary caregiver. She speaks openly about the isolation and fatigue that come as the illness reaches its worst stages. Her willingness to unzip her soul is what makes reading this book so helpful. Her insights speak to emotional and spiritual-health issues that arise every day. And—this is so significant—she highlights the importance of supportive friends and family for remaining resilient.

I honor my friend for trying so hard to be thankful for what she had with her husband rather than emphasizing what was being lost as the disease ravaged Bob's mind. This was overcoming with faith, not just surviving.

Bob Fantasia has been gone for two years now. On the first anniversary of his death, Cynthia and her family invited about thirty people to a special luncheon. These people had been especially present to the Fantasias during Bob's illness. The family wanted to express gratitude for the ways they had been loved during those difficult years. As people came together that day, there was laughter, singing, and sharing stories of the grace of God in Bob and Cynthia's lives. It was an unforgettable occasion in which people acknowledged the difference it makes when people know how to love each other and enter each other's most painful seasons.

You are in for an insightful experience. Cynthia Fantasia describes what it is like to walk through so much pain and loss, yet—at the same time—find the lingering light of God's presence. Thank you, Cynthia, my friend, for the great gift of this book.

Gail MacDonald

CHAPTER 1

BEGINNING THE JOURNEY

Relying on God has to begin all over again
every day as if nothing yet had been done.

C. S. LEWIS, *Letters to Malcolm: Chiefly on Prayer*

IT WAS A SUNNY January day, and we were heading to
the doctor for Bob's appointment. Just an ordinary
appointment—nothing to worry about. Sure, he had been
acting a little "off" lately: a bit forgetful, asking the same
questions over and over, unable to remember names or
dates. But everyone has those problems, don't they? He
was a bit depressed—the world had changed, and his skills
weren't in demand anymore. He was worried about his
favorite aunt because she was old and not doing well. He
was just trying to "find" himself.

Or, at least, that's what I told myself.

I was upbeat. I was planning to retire in six months, and we were going to do all the things we just hadn't had time to do: spend more time with our grandchildren, take long beach walks on our beloved Maine coast, perhaps sell our home to begin condo living. I would read those books that had been piling up and have rich conversations with Bob and friends over leisurely cups of coffee. Yes, life held such promise. Nothing would go wrong!

I had lived a happy life. For twenty-four years, I served as pastor of women for Grace Chapel, a large and vibrant church in the heart of historic Lexington, Massachusetts. My career had given me the unexpected opportunity to become a world traveler. If there was an opportunity to go, I did—with Bob's full support and encouragement. And I went without a care, because he was so capable. We tend to accept our happy lives and think they'll always be that way.

Bob had been retired for a few years and was adjusting well. He enjoyed puttering around in the yard and chatting with the neighbors or with anyone who happened to walk by. His career in the environmental field had taken him around the country as he offered consultation in this cutting-edge industry. When not traveling, he taught classes at church to adults who were exploring faith, and his nonjudgmental and lighthearted manner drew many closer to the Lord. He also served for many years as an elder, and his endearing ways made him approachable to all.

But then, there was the forgetfulness.

CHANGES

"I'm going to say three things," the doctor told Bob. "Red. Sunshine. New York." They went on chatting for a short time. I repeated those three words over and over in my mind. "Okay, Bob," the doctor asked, "what were those three words I told you a few minutes ago?"

I was ready with the answer. But when I glanced at Bob, I saw him looking blankly—first at the doctor, and then at me.

After an awkward moment, the doctor moved on to some other cognitive tests. Bob failed each one.

"It appears to be a classic case of Alzheimer's disease." I heard the doctor's words, but they seemed to be echoing from a deep tunnel. Bob seemingly heard nothing, still displaying his warm, engaging smile. *God's mercy*, I thought.

Alzheimer's disease is an ugly, tragic disease. At this point, there is no cure. Best estimates are that a new case of Alzheimer's is diagnosed in America about every seventy seconds. It is not a normal part of aging.

Our son brought it up first. I was not totally surprised, but a bit stunned. It was one of those things when you really only see the signs in retrospect, as if through a rearview mirror. Because my husband was so high functioning, the diagnosis was a gradual unfolding, a very long dusk before impending (though certain) darkness.

—LAURA

Alzheimer's disease (AD) is a progressive, degenerative disorder that attacks the brain's nerve cells, or neurons, resulting in loss of memory, thinking and language skills, and behavioral changes. AD is the most common cause of dementia, or loss of intellectual function, among people aged 65 and older.[1]

As the doctor spoke, my heart raced. Yet, at the same time, I felt an unusual calm come over me. I met with the doctor while Bob sat with our daughters in the waiting room. "What can I expect? What's the progression of the disease? What kind of a time line are we talking about?"

"I just can't say. I can give you general answers, but each person is so different, there are no definitive answers." A response that my type A personality didn't want to hear.

The doctor had a question for me: "How are you going to handle all of this?"

There I sat, a follower of Christ, somehow trying to balance the reality of all the pain Alzheimer's disease would inflict on us with the hope of God's care and eternal life in heaven. Without thinking, I responded, "I guess I'm going to live on the other side of eternity." I would do my best to focus on the eternal, to trust the One who held eternity in His hands, the One who had gone ahead to prepare a place for us and would come back to take us to be with Him (John 14:3).

I had no idea how many times those words would pierce my heart and remind me where my focus had to be. When you are in the pit of caring for someone with Alzheimer's, it is a daily challenge to look beyond the pain to the hope of eternity.

We walked out of the hospital different people than when we had walked in.

FOG

Bob was fine—just another doctor's appointment. "I told you I was fine," he laughed.

But I wasn't fine. A shroud of gray, a deep fog, seemed to be rolling toward me. Slowly, it marked its path and began enveloping me. Our daughters were quiet. As we walked to the parking garage, cars whizzed by us and an ambulance careened toward the hospital, but we seemed to be walking in an alternate universe. Bob was chattering away and the sun was shining, but sounds were muffled, and all I could see was gray.

David was having problems crunching grades for his college students. There were other problems also, yet the doctors could not figure out what was wrong. He was seen by a neurologist and diagnosed with frontal lobe dementia. I was stunned. My father had died after a long battle with Alzheimer's. I knew this was going to be bad.

—LORRAINE

That night, after Bob went to bed, I cried out to the Lord. I didn't ask "Why?" Instead I asked "How?"

Alzheimer's disease had become an unwelcome guest in our lives, and its presence would grow with each passing day. It felt as if we were jumping in the car and leaving on a road trip without even knowing our destination. How would I navigate this uncertain road before us? How would I make the right decisions for Bob? How could I protect his dignity and provide proper care?

That fog remained, my ever-present companion. I longed to wake up from this nightmare and resume my life as I knew and loved it.

As I sobbed, it seemed as if God heard me and brought Abraham to my mind and heart.

> The LORD had said to Abram, "Go from your country, your people and your father's household to the land I will show you." . . . So Abram went, as the LORD had told him.
>
> GENESIS 12:1, 4

The Lord clearly told Abraham that He was sending him away from all that was familiar and comfortable. Abraham would leave the land, the people, and the family that he knew and loved. He would go to a place he knew nothing about, to people he didn't know. And, other than his immediate family, all Abraham would have to rely on was God.

I could certainly relate. Just that afternoon, I had been told that I would embark on a journey that I knew nothing about, would travel a road that was very uncertain, and would most likely have my heart broken on a daily basis.

A GOOD WORD

Many years before, when Bob and I were going through a crisis, a friend had shared, "There is no chaos in heaven about this." God was not then, nor is He now, sitting in heaven scratching His head, asking, "How did I miss this?" For this new crisis as for that earlier one, there was no chaos in heaven.

He promised me in His Word:

- I shouldn't fear because He is with me (Isaiah 41:10).
- He will never leave me or forsake me (Hebrews 13:5).
- He knew that I was scared—that I was discouraged: "Be strong and courageous. Do not be afraid; do not be discouraged, for the LORD your God will be with you wherever you go" (Joshua 1:9).

As I thought about these verses, it became clear that I had to choose, on a daily basis, where to place my trust. Would I travel this uncertain road with the One who created the universe, who created me (and Bob), who knows the future because He has already been there? Or would I creep along in the dark, hoping to do the right thing and take the correct turns?

My decision was soon made. There was no choice.

If the shadow of Alzheimer's has turned your world upside down, please remember that the light of God's presence and care will never dim.

The next six months leading to my retirement were exceptionally difficult. I scrambled to find people who would "visit" with Bob for long periods of time so I could work. He had suddenly become confused—not totally, but enough that I didn't dare leave him at home alone.

While we were on a trip to Colorado, I became aware of my husband's confusion and forgetfulness. Upon returning home, we realized he had left his keys at security in Denver. We clung to the hope that his memory issues were due to a vitamin deficiency, but a neurologist confirmed that we were on the Alzheimer's path.

—SARAH

I was blessed with a very understanding supervisor who assured me that I could work from home as needed. But the demands of an active ministry were exhausting. Preparing a Bible-study lecture each week became more draining than energizing. And having my physical body in one place while my mind and heart were in another was bankrupting my soul.

Finally, the big day arrived: I exited the office and my exciting professional life . . . to begin my new career as a full-time caregiver.

And so our journey began, one fog-filled step at a time, with no knowledge of what each day would bring.

Four years passed between the day of diagnosis and Bob's death. There were days and nights—moments when I wanted to just pack it all up. Would I have chosen this path for my life? Of course not. But would I have passed up the lessons that I learned (and am still learning), the love and help from family and friends, and the deep growth in me? Absolutely not!

A doctor friend wrote words that I carried in my heart throughout our journey:

There's a period of time between . . . diagnosis and the moment when a life ends, and that entire period of time contains life. Sometimes this time is months, sometimes it's years, sometimes it's weeks. Far too often we . . . are so distracted by the perceived inevitability of death that the life contained therein passes by, and sometimes we forget to live it.[2]

In the reality of our sad, uncertain journey ahead, I decided that I would do my best to savor and celebrate the life that Bob and I would have together—in spite of, and in the presence of, Alzheimer's disease. Don't let the diagnosis and your circumstances crush you. The shadow will always be there, but there are moments of joy and memories still to be made. Look for ways to savor and celebrate!

DISNEY WORLD

There would be no move to a condo. We were moving to "Disney World"—the Alzheimer's world of fantasy and forgotten memories in which Bob would find comfort, and where I would need to find some form of peace. In a way, "Disney World" became my slogan, a daily reminder that my life, as I had planned it, had come to an abrupt halt. Bob believed he was fine, so would I spend the time we had together correcting Bob's "reality" or going along with it?

The choice to go along with it, to "live in Disney World," proved to be a good one for both of us. I would do the season well (as far as it depended on me), trusting the One who would (and did) always strengthen and lead me.

This is the book I never wanted to write. I had a plethora of book ideas in my head and heart for many years. Somehow, the ideas never found their way to a computer. If you are reading this book as a caregiver to a loved one with the disease, if you know someone who is a caregiver or has been diagnosed, or if you have been touched in some way by the damage done by Alzheimer's, I am writing to you.

From diagnosis to my husband's death, I walked a lonely and isolated road, far different from the life I had enjoyed. Throughout our journey, though, there were people who chose to walk with us. There was also the continual assurance of God's presence and faithfulness, along with little illuminations or discoveries that would help to make this journey easier. My hope for *Lingering Light* is that it will offer you some light for the next step or two, that you will know you are part of a huge chorus of brothers and sisters who are on this journey, and that my story will give you strength and brighten your day.

As I began to write, I realized that my story is just that, my story. In the sidebars throughout this book, you will read snippets of experiences from what I call traveling companions. Some of these are people I know personally, others are friends of friends. Each was eager to share her story with me.[3]

"Traveling Light" sections are nuggets of truth that I gathered throughout my journey. I learned that I had to focus on my husband and his needs, but also, I needed to care for myself. Caregivers can't be weighed down by unnecessary burdens or overly busy schedules. You can tuck these nuggets into your heart and ponder them in a spare moment. They are meant to help you focus and prepare for another step in your journey.

I read short devotionals throughout Bob's illness, found lots of quotations (I love quotes) that encouraged me and gave me insight, and loved reading prayers that spoke to the struggle I was experiencing. I share them with you in the hope that they will encourage you, lighten your burden, and brighten your day, as they did for me.

My journey now is a new one—learning to live as a single person. It is a challenging journey. But I believe with all my heart that nothing in life is wasted, and I pray that you will find hope in these pages, that you will see your loved one with new eyes, and that you will find strength for the days ahead.

Write in this book. Share your heart. Compose your own prayer. God is listening, and His light is lingering.

Traveling Light

A dementia diagnosis starts you on an unexpected and unknown trajectory. But "that entire period of time contains life." Plan for a demanding trip, but leave time to savor the journey. Trust the One who knows the way.

A Prayer to Guide You

O God, our heavenly Father, whose glory fills the whole creation, and whose presence we find wherever we go: Preserve those who travel; surround them with your loving care; protect them from every danger; and bring them in safety to their journey's end; through Jesus Christ our Lord. Amen.

THE BOOK OF COMMON PRAYER

CHAPTER 2

ASKING FOR DIRECTIONS

If ever there's a tomorrow when we're not together,
there's something you must remember. . . . You're
braver than you believe, and stronger than
you seem, and smarter than you think.

CHRISTOPHER ROBIN TO WINNIE THE POOH,
Pooh's Grand Adventure

MOST OF MY PROFESSIONAL LIFE was spent giving instructions, directions, and advice. As a teacher, I stood in front
of classes of anxious students eager to learn (or at least
eager to follow my direction to earn a good grade). As a
pastor, I counseled countless folks seemingly wandering
in their own sea of confusion. I lectured in front of hun-
dreds of women, helping them apply biblical truths to their
lives. I was the featured speaker at retreats and conferences;
people actually paid money to listen to my advice! Now

I had embarked on a new journey and had no idea where I was going or how I was going to get there. And I had no advice to give myself. I was the one who had to ask for directions. Who do I ask? What do I ask?

Bob remained happy and content. Nothing in his life had changed; he considered himself healthy, living in the home he loved, pruning every shrub and flowering bush in the yard, and watching his favorite TV shows. But my life had changed dramatically. Bob couldn't be left alone, so he accompanied me on every errand. He asked me the same questions over and over, and he would announce when it was time to take a walk and when it was time to eat. It didn't take me very long to realize that this arrangement was not sustainable—for me or for him.

I, the direction giver, now had to be the direction receiver.

I could certainly relate to King Jehoshaphat, a direction giver who was under attack by surrounding enemy armies whose sole purpose was to destroy him and his people (2 Chronicles 20:1-30). It seemed as if everything surrounding me was similarly out of control and that I was in a battle for my (and Bob's) very life! Jehoshaphat and his army were overwhelmed, outnumbered, and filled with fear. I was too.

Sometimes when the heart cries out in fear, the head has to remind the heart that God is still in control and has not abandoned us. So when Jehoshaphat cried out, "We have no power to face this vast army that is attacking us. We do not know what to do, but our eyes are on you" (2 Chronicles 20:12), God responded, "Do not be afraid;

do not be discouraged. Go out to face them tomorrow, and the LORD will be with you" (verse 17).

Taking my cues from Jehoshaphat's prayer, I prayed:

You are Creator and Sustainer of the entire universe. You hold all the power and are in control of all the events in my life. But, Lord, I am in a place I know nothing about, and I'm not sure where or how to begin. I feel so alone and so weak. I do not know what to do, but my eyes are on you!

And just as God directed Jehoshaphat, He did the same for me: "Go out and face them, Cynthia. I, your Lord, will be with you."

I would smile sadly and often—usually once a day— when I thought of the interchange between Alice and the Cheshire Cat in *Alice's Adventures in Wonderland.*

"Would you tell me, please, which way I ought to walk from here?"

"That depends a good deal on where you want to get to," said the Cat.

"I don't much care where—" said Alice.

"Then it doesn't matter which way you go," said the Cat. . . .

"—so long as I get SOMEWHERE," Alice added as an explanation.

"Oh, you're sure to do that," said the Cat, "if you only walk long enough."[4]

Like Alice, I needed to ask for directions, not knowing (and often not caring, beyond getting through the day) where I was going. Also, like Alice, I didn't have to know the specifics of what was ahead. When I felt lost, I just had to keep moving and trust God to daily shine His light on my darkening path.

A friend reminded me recently of something I told her early in my journey—words I had forgotten but she remembered because she is now on this same dark road with her husband. I told her I had two goals in my life:

1. to preserve Bob's dignity, and
2. to preserve my sanity.

The questions I asked of others, and of God, were based on these two goals.

PRESERVING BOB'S DIGNITY

Bob had been a wonderful provider for our family, and that had allowed me to enjoy an incredibly winsome life. But when checks were returned, bills were not paid, and the mail didn't arrive (I later found some of his hiding places—no wonder the bills didn't get paid!), there was no denying that we were in trouble. And I had no idea how to begin addressing the situation. Bob was unwilling to release the responsibility of writing checks, so I told him that I wanted to learn and asked him to teach me. He was pleased about that, and while he "explained" how to write a check, I just wrote out the checks, asking him to seal the envelope and affix the stamp. The day came when he was no longer able to even seal and stamp. One more heartache.

Because Bob had always taken care of these details, I needed to figure out what questions even needed to be asked. Which meant I had to learn to swallow my pride and ask.

I started by asking friends where they did their banking, who their financial planner was, and a variety of other things. I needed to set up a new checking account. The woman at the bank was incredibly helpful and compassionate. As soon as I explained my situation, she not only helped to set up a checking account but also addressed and resolved a variety of other issues. Thank you, Lord! A new financial planner took care of the details of my retirement years. He prayed with me at the end of each session. Thank you, Lord! Our lawyer had been our friend for years. He attended to every legal issue that I was facing and freed me from worrying about what-ifs. Thank you, Lord!

> *It hasn't been easy for my mom caring for my dad. She's spent countless hours at appointments, on the phone, and dealing with insurance companies. It seems cruel how the caregiver is left to navigate all of these business-world issues while struggling to come to grips with the diagnosis.*
> —HANNAH

I realize that this is not the case for everyone. In fact, my situation was the outlier. It is important to search until you find the right person for the right task. Most towns have a Council on Aging that is well-resourced to help you locate the help you need.

The more caregivers I talk with, the more I learn that the financial and legal issues are the areas that weigh the heaviest. A friend shared the following story with me:

Finding the right doctors and medical support was one of the greatest struggles my dad and I faced. My mom's doctor did not catch this terrible disease anywhere near early enough. Thus, we felt passed around from one doctor and neurologist to another.

—KELLY

It wasn't just that Roger was "going away" from Ann as his dementia increased. She had papers on her desk that she couldn't deal with: a $1,200 bill for Roger's ambulance trip, which said, "Please forward this to your health insurance company. In absence of insurance, you will be personally obligated to cover this expense." Ann had no idea which company provided their health insurance—or where Roger kept the info. And Roger no longer knew either.

As I look back on our journey, I realize that I should have asked Bob more questions much earlier, gotten more direction from him while he still remembered. This is important for every caregiver to understand and address.

PRESERVING MY SANITY

The Alzheimer's Association provides guidance and direction for caregivers.

• Know what community resources are available.

- Get help and find support.
- Use relaxation techniques.
- Get moving.
- Find time for yourself.
- Become an educated caregiver.
- Take care of yourself.
- Make legal and financial plans.[5]

Each of the above can be tailored to meet an individual caregiver's needs. Choose the areas where you are struggling, pray, then begin looking for practical steps you can take. I didn't utilize every item, but I did find this information very helpful. This part of our journey was incredibly difficult, and I in no way want to make it sound like it was easy. But take heart; you're going to make it.

At this point, I had the primary responsibility of getting her medical care and taking her to various doctor's appointments. She had six different doctors—these appointments kept me busy.

—Louise

Once a caregiver enters the medical maze of Alzheimer's, the emotional and physical toll grows for both the caregiver and the loved one. I continue talking with many caregivers, and they tell me that their journey through the medical world was as exhausting as caring for their loved one. The people we depend on to ask questions to and receive guidance from are now the very ones also caught up in the maze, the ones who cause the most confusion. Bob and I were blessed to have had a wonderful community of medical folks who lovingly guided us even when they didn't necessarily have the answers I hoped for. But I know that is not the norm, and for that, my heart is heavy.

This was probably the most stretching experience during my role as caregiver: No one could answer my questions—probably because there were no answers.

EVEN WONDER WOMAN NEEDS HELP

Life requires some rest stops—to stretch your legs, get some refreshment, and ask for updated directions. A twenty-four-hours-a-day, seven-days-a-week job is exhausting! I needed some time to be alone, to think, to breathe, to just rest.

In what would gradually become our new normal, I had to swallow my pride and ask for directions. I wasn't Wonder Woman. I had to accept the truth that in order for me to continue caring for Bob, I had to rest—which meant that I had to trust others to care for Bob.

Aside from family and friends, two caregivers (who became dear friends) each gave me a weekly five-hour break: precious time to read, enjoy lunch with a friend, listen to the silence, and allow my spirit to catch up with my body.

It's a jolt to anyone's psyche to realize *I cannot do this task alone. The days ahead are going to get harder, and my loved one is going to get worse.* Perhaps you are feeling this way right now. Please remember, as I learned, asking for directions isn't a sign of failure. It's a sign of strength and a willingness to journey on!

Traveling Light

Alzheimer's disease affects the caregiver as well as the patient. Feelings of inadequacy, fear, and hopelessness begin to cloud your thinking. Finding the best resources will give you peace of mind and confidence for the next leg of the journey.

A Prayer to Guide You

Lord, thank You for the people You have divinely placed in my life who speak holy truth, love and words of wisdom. Give me a heart of discernment to know when You are using someone to speak instruction into my heart and my circumstances, and give me the strength and courage to follow through with that advice, even when it's hard. Fill me with peace in knowing that even if I take a wrong turn, Your purpose will prevail. In Jesus' Name, Amen.

TRACIE MILES,
A prayer for godly wisdom, proverbs31.org

CHAPTER 3

NIGHT

Too many of us panic in the dark. We don't understand that it's a holy dark and that the idea is to surrender to it and journey through to real light.

SUE MONK KIDD, *When the Heart Waits*

"IT'S WEDNESDAY," I told Bob.

"So what?" he responded.

"Well, Bill is coming to go for a walk and have lunch with you."

"Who's Bill?" Bob queried.

We were about a year into our Alzheimer's journey, and the darkness continued to envelop us—the same questions, the same answers, every day. The changes were subtle, yet the losses were great. I tried to be patient and helpful, but the darkness kept rolling in and the frustration kept building. Bill was a good friend from church who came every other Wednesday. He and Bob would walk, enjoy lunch, and talk—the same conversation each time.

Those Wednesdays became precious to me. Bill gave me some time alone to collapse in a chair, listen to the quiet, clear my head, and try to see my life a bit more clearly.

A HOLY DARK

I have never been a fan of darkness. As a young child, I'd ask my dad to check all the nooks and crannies in my room to be certain they were free from all things that lurk in the night. Grateful that a streetlamp shone outside my bedroom window, I often needed an additional night-light to chase away the monsters and shadows that were my companions until I fell asleep.

Now I was an adult. The shadows and monsters were real, and their name was Alzheimer's disease. Where was my night-light? Where was my streetlamp? I was unable to move because I couldn't see where to go.

But this adult fear was different. I was not afraid of the monsters that were "out there" but of the monsters that were in me: monsters of inadequacy, the need to know the schedule, the need to control, the need to know the end of the story *now*, so I could handle the future.

This darkness, this night, was something I could have done without, but here it was, and I was right in the

It took months for the diagnosis to really sink in and then more months for all of us to process it. Truly, even with all my mom's symptoms, I don't think her diagnosis became real until about two years prior to her death. When the hospital bed arrived at the house, things started becoming very real.

—KELLY

middle of it. I wanted to believe that I would grow from this experience—even in the heartache of it all. I found myself wondering whether God would guide me through the dark, offer His grace, and show me His love.

Most caregivers I talk with cautiously share the same concerns. Is God big enough to handle this? To have patience with us? Will He stand by His promise to never leave or forsake us (Deuteronomy 31:6)? These are tough questions, and caregivers ask them in the dark. It takes time to understand and trust the darkness, to comprehend a God so big yet so personal, to open ourselves up to His grace and power. And it only happens when we let Him into our darkness and give Him permission to transform it into a "holy dark," where He will grow and shape us, draw us close to Him, and send His light to guide us.

THE FACTS OF ALZHEIMER'S DARKNESS

Alzheimer's and other forms of dementia are diagnoses of individuals, but they have an undeniable family impact: They open a range of needs and vulnerabilities among all those in close relationship to the person given the diagnosis.

And the statistics were not helpful when I thought about the future and my seeming lack of control.

According to the Alzheimer's Association's "2018 Alzheimer's Facts and Figures,"

- Nearly two thirds of those with Alzheimer's at age seventy are expected to die before they turn eighty.

- Alzheimer's disease is officially listed as the sixth-leading cause of death in the United States overall. For people past the age of sixty-five it is the fifth-leading cause of death.
- As the population of the United States ages, Alzheimer's is becoming a more common cause of death. "Between 2000 and 2015, deaths from Alzheimer's disease as recorded on death certificates increased 123 percent, while deaths from the number one cause of death (heart disease) decreased 11 percent."
- Every sixty-five seconds a new person develops Alzheimer's. Within forty years that rate will increase to one new victim every 33 seconds.
- "Alzheimer's disease is the only top ten cause of death in the United States that cannot be prevented, cured or even slowed."[6]

The future didn't look very bright, certainly not filled with a whole lot of hope. Perhaps that's the way your future looks right now. How does someone manage a journey with so many unknowns? How would I navigate through a role reversal, now that I was responsible for a loved one who used to take care of everything? These questions and others loomed large in front of me. I prayed for guidance. I had much to learn.

The high school our son attended was a campus with several classroom buildings, some quite a distance from others. Prior to the first "Back-to-School Night," all parents received a letter explaining the evening's schedule.

Two important instructions came at the end of the letter: (1) wear comfortable shoes, and (2) bring a flashlight. *Odd instructions*, I thought. That night, as we walked down dark paths, climbed narrow stairs, and maneuvered tricky passages, I was grateful I had followed instructions. What struck me the most was this: The beam of light from my flashlight was not enough to light up the entire campus, but it was enough to light the next step in front of me.

Henri Nouwen has good advice for all of us:

Often we want to be able to see into the future. We say, "How will next year be for me? Where will I be five or ten years from now?" There are no answers to these questions. Mostly we have just enough light to see the next step: what we have to do in the coming hour or the following day. The art of living is to enjoy what we can see and not complain about what remains in the dark. When we are able to take the next step with the trust that we will have enough light for the step that follows, we can walk through life with joy and be surprised at how far we go. Let's rejoice in the little light we carry and not ask for the great beam that would take all shadows away.[7]

The psalmist reminds us that God's Word "is a lamp for my feet, a light on my path" (Psalm 119:105). It was true on that back-to-school night many years ago, and it is true for us today, no matter in what season of darkness we find ourselves.

In the book of Joshua, we read how Joshua became the

leader of the Israelites. Moses had died, and a new leader was needed to guide God's people across the Jordan River and into the Promised Land. God explained the details of their journey, and then He gave Joshua a command and a promise:

My dad received his mild cognitive impairment diagnosis, which I immediately interpreted as Alzheimer's and a death sentence, the day my husband and I brought our third son home from the hospital. I crumbled and spent the afternoon sobbing. I thought my dad, age sixty-two, would never get to know this new grandson of his.

—HANNAH

Be strong and courageous. Do not be afraid; do not be discouraged, for the LORD your God will be with you wherever you go.

JOSHUA 1:9

Nowhere in this story do we read that Joshua told God he was afraid. But God knew. Caring for an Alzheimer's loved one can be scary at times, and most of us have moments when we are afraid. I certainly did. But God's Word was true for Joshua, and it is true for us. This is a season that requires strength and courage. But it is also a season when God is with us wherever we go.

A FRIEND IN THE DARK

God's light for each day comes from His Word and His presence. That gave me comfort. But there are lots of tears in the dark. Sometimes, as a child, I would cry myself to sleep in the dark because I was afraid. Now, as an adult,

I would run to the bathroom, turn on the faucet, and let the tears flow—because I was afraid. As a child, I felt so alone. Now as an adult, I felt alone, but Bob was still with me . . . or was he?

I love the words to the song "Weep with Me" by Rend Collective:

> *Weep with me*
> *Lord, will You weep with me?*
> *I don't need answers, all I need*
> *Is to know that You care for me.*[8]

My husband had been a great comforter, but now I felt so alone.

I learned that God often sends people (friends, caregivers) to speak words of hope and comfort. Liz was a neighbor and friend. Our kids had been school friends, and her husband had died from Alzheimer's disease five years earlier. She was my go-to person when I had questions about Bob.

It seemed that Liz would show up at my door just when I needed her. "Am I going to make it?" I would ask her.

She would respond, "Yup, but it'll be hard. You'll be different at the end of your journey. But you will make it."

When I thought I had blown it, Liz would encourage me by saying, "What you are feeling is normal. I used to feel the same way. Bob looks great, and he seems so happy. You're doing a great job making him feel secure and safe." Her words were like a balm to my weary soul and oxygen to my lungs. I could be real with Liz. She was truly a light on my path.

GLIMMERS OF HOPE

Sometimes it was just a peaceful moment, a cardinal sitting on our deck, a beautiful sunset, or a card from a friend that would give me a glimmer of hope. In my other life, before Alzheimer's, I wouldn't have given these things much thought. But now they became reminders of God's kindness and love.

How do we as caregivers train our eyes to see God in these little incidents—especially when so much of our energy is going to noticing and addressing the tough stuff happening in our loved one's life? If you are not a caregiver but know someone who is, don't underestimate the gift you can give by simply sending a card. (Two things that don't help: [1] stopping by unannounced and staying too long, and [2] expecting long conversations on the phone.)

One bright winter morning, when the snowdrifts were high, Bob looked out our family room window and announced, "Look, there are some beautiful red flowers growing out of the snow!"

Oh boy, I thought as I went to join him at the window. *Things are getting bad.* Sure enough, however, several red tulips were poking through the snowdrift. It turned out that our friend Judy had driven by late the night before and planted the lovely silk tulips. They truly brightened our day. Simple, short, and life-giving.

One of the saddest days early in this journey (I had no

idea of the sadder days to come) was when the doctor told Bob he could no longer drive. Although the news did not register with Bob, it certainly registered with me. What was I to do? How could I explain this to a man who wasn't understanding much of anything?

Once again, Liz came to the rescue. She just happened to walk by our home that afternoon. Bob was out in the backyard, so she and I could talk. Because Bob was always losing things, Liz suggested that I hide his truck key. (Actually, I found those keys a year after Bob died—even I had forgotten where I hid them!) Then Liz suggested that we call our friend at the car dealership and ask if he would help me.

Just as Liz was leaving, Bob came in the house and said to her, "They said I can't drive because I'm too old."

"You're not old, Bob," Liz lovingly responded. "But that truck—that's old!" Just the right response, and Bob nodded his head and laughed.

The next morning, I drove my car around the block, pulled over on a side street and made the call to the car dealer. I explained the situation and the doctor's order. "Rob, would you take a look at Bob's truck and tell him it would be too expensive to repair?" I apologized for drawing him into this intrigue. But he responded, "I'm happy to help out. Do you have any idea how many spouses have called me to do the same for their loved one?" I was so relieved, so grateful, so teary.

Rob then said, "I'll tell Bob that when the weather gets nice, I'll take him to look at some new trucks."

Sure enough, later that morning, Bob tried to start

the truck with his house key. It broke my heart to watch him struggle, but the plan was in place. He came in to tell me that his truck was broken. I told him I'd call and get it towed to the dealership. As the tow truck pulled into our driveway, who drove in behind the tow truck? Rob.

What caused me to fall apart were the endless repeated questions and stories in the early years. It was so frustrating for me at first, before I realized that correcting her was pointless. Once I finally realized that it was nothing my mom could control, that it was the disease talking, I tried finding creative ways to respond.

—Donna

Liz called these little maneuvers "fiblets"—a way of mitigating our loved one's anxiety where attempting to reason with them might elevate their stress. If we try to reason with people living with dementia, we only make them anxious. We'll never convince them, because reality is no longer clear to them.

I would continue to use fiblets with Bob to lessen his anxiety and maintain his dignity. If Bob got frustrated because he couldn't remember a name or what he had for breakfast, I would say, "Oh, I know. Sometimes I can't remember things either."

One morning, I brought Bob his shower kit, but he was exasperated. "I can't," he said. "Those three people who live upstairs locked the bathroom door."

Of course, no one was living upstairs. "Okay," I responded, "I'll go unlock it." And with a paper clip in hand, I went upstairs, picked the lock, and opened the bathroom door. Bob happily went in and took his shower.

GOD WAS NEAR

I had a choice. How did I want this journey to end? It was so early in this journey, and yet it was so dark. Slowly I came to realize that the darkness could be a holy dark because I was not alone. God was near.

> Whoever dwells in the shelter of the Most High
>> will rest in the shadow of the Almighty.
> I will say of the LORD, "He is my refuge and my
>> fortress,
>> my God, in whom I trust."
> He will cover you with His feathers,
>> and under his wings you will find refuge;
> his faithfulness will be your shield and
>> rampart.
>
> PSALM 91:1-2, 4

I chose to take God at His word. I was in a safe place, hidden under His wings, protected by His grace, and guided by His Word, His presence, and His people. I would trust God for the future (although I still had no idea what that was going to look like) and focus on the task before me, loving and caring for my husband one day— sometimes one hour—at a time. I would move forward until the night became dawn.

Traveling Light

Darkness is part of the Alzheimer's journey. We caregivers can continue to grope in the night or grab hold of God's hand. Sometimes His hand comes in the form of a friend, God's Word, or just the abiding light of His presence.

A Prayer to Guide You

Father, I am weary, but I struggle to rest, to sleep. The darkness increases my fears because I can't see the road ahead. I want answers; I want control; I want peace. Yet I am learning that You want me to surrender—surrender to You, my light in the dark night. I lift my hand to You and ask that You grab hold and lead me through this darkness. The night always gives way to dawn, and I will hold tight until the light comes—when and how, I do not know. But I know that You know the unknown, You are sovereign, and You love me. Lead me and guide me, I pray.

CYNTHIA FANTASIA

CHAPTER 4

TRAVELING ESSENTIALS

*The key is this: Meet today's problems with today's
strength. Don't start tackling tomorrow's problems
until tomorrow. You do not have tomorrow's
strength yet. You simply have enough for today.*

MAX LUCADO, *Traveling Light*

I AM SITTING LAKESIDE at my son's summer home in Maine.
The water is lapping the rocks by the shore. I am listening
to the squeals and giggles of my grandchildren cannon-
balling off the dock, vying for the biggest splash. The
cloudless sky and bright sunshine envelop me in a warm
blanket of contentment. Although I am here for only a few
days, I have brought enough clothes and toiletries for a few
months. After all, the weather may change, my shoes may
get wet, and something may get dirty. So I pack for the
what-ifs, telling myself it is better to be prepared than to go
without.

As I sit in this beautiful setting and think about the "essentials" I brought with me for this short stay, my mind wanders to Abigail. I have always loved the story of Abigail. She is my role model. When Abigail learned that David was planning to kill her husband and all the men in his family, she quickly set a plan in motion. In 1 Samuel 25:18 we read:

The caregiver must figure out a way to pursue life-giving activities. If that's Bible study and devotionals, do them. If it's spending time with friends, do that—especially with ones who understand that they are needed.

—Joan

Abigail . . . took two hundred loaves of bread, two skins of wine, five dressed sheep, five seahs of roasted grain, a hundred cakes of raisins and two hundred cakes of pressed figs, and loaded them on donkeys.

After presenting the food to David and his troops, Abigail appealed to David's sense of responsibility: He must not carry out his plan to kill Nabal. David took her advice. God was the one to intervene on David's behalf, and David's good name was preserved.

We learn from this story that Abigail was prepared for anything, with adequate resources for even the most unlikely contingency. What is essential to life as a caregiver to someone with dementia? It's less about stuff and more about attitude. The capacity to pivot as needs change, the faith that the unexpected will not devastate you, that God will provide even in the most stressful circumstances—these are more critical than a stocked refrigerator.

This was a challenging lesson for me, one I didn't learn overnight. What was absolutely necessary for this journey? The answers came in surprising ways.

FRUSTRATION MARKED MANY DAYS

Most of my days caring for Bob were marked with tension and frustration. I missed my old life and wanted it back. I clung to the way we had lived, my fingers wrapped tightly around familiar things I thought were important. My patience wore thin, and my words escaped before my brain edited them.

One morning, very early, I stumbled into the kitchen to get a drink of water. Half asleep, it took me a few seconds to realize that my feet were wet. I looked up and spied the freezer door, wide open. Water was dripping down the front of the refrigerator, onto the floor, and making its way directly to my bare feet. As I stood there, it suddenly registered: ice cream (with the lid off the carton), meat, vegetables, ice cubes—everything—wasted.

I was speechless and horrified. When had this happened? Why hadn't I heard Bob get up? What was I going to do? Was this what my future was going to be like?

I began by closing the freezer door. Then, in slow motion, I dried my feet, wiped up the water on the floor, got a large trash bag, and emptied the contents of the freezer. I never asked Bob what had happened. He was sleeping peacefully, and I knew he didn't have any answers.

In an email to a dear friend, the first summer after Bob's diagnosis, I wrote:

Just returned from a meeting with Bob's doctor (without Bob). I "meet" with him by phone each week, but this time he suggested we meet face-to-face. He is concerned about me (caregiver), and today he was lovingly direct. I have seen a sharp decline in Bob's mental acuity. He appears fine but has a terrible time with word retrieval, names, relationships, and memory retention. He is becoming more dependent on me, and I see (even though he tries to cover it up) an increasing insecurity about lots of things. He is still his sweet self but is truly unable to carry on any kind of meaningful conversation. Where does he do best? With the grandkids. They have all noticed something is not right with him, but they are still loving and happy when they are around Bob. He seems to engage well with them—at their level.

So, all of the above gives you a picture of what is happening here. My heart is broken as I continue to say small good-byes to the stuff that made up our life together. I am grateful for a seasoned faith, although sometimes I do question His confidence in me to travel this journey.

I am taking it one day at a time, but the doctor told me I need to begin to put some plans in place in order to take care of myself. So, everything is on hold; I can't make plans, can't look ahead, just need to take one day at a time. And you know how hard that is for me. The other night as I shut down my computer, I just put my head in my lap and said, "Lord, I feel so useless!" There is just no way to prepare the heart for this kind of experience—to watch the love of your life 'shrink' before your very eyes, to be unable to do anything to change it, to not know what these next months will bring—or how long this will go on. I just keep asking the Lord to be merciful—to both of us.

One of the earliest lessons came through an argument Bob and I had. I don't remember what the argument was about, but more than likely it was about my unrealistic expectations of what our life should be like at this time in our lives. At one point, Bob stormed out of the room, leaving me still angry and talking to myself.

About five minutes later, Bob returned with a big smile on his face, put his arm around me, and said, "Honey, want to take a walk?" He had totally forgotten we had had an argument, was eager to do something with me, and was in a wonderful mood.

I had to make a choice: continue to be angry or take a walk. We took a walk around our neighborhood—holding hands as we went.

Do not let any unwholesome talk come out of your mouths, but only what is helpful for building others up according to their needs. . . . Get rid of all bitterness, rage and anger, brawling and slander, along with every form of malice. Be kind and compassionate to one another, forgiving each other, just as in Christ God forgave you.

EPHESIANS 4:29, 31-32

My husband, an Alzheimer's patient, lived these words. I thought deeply about how this could be. I discovered that he didn't just start living this way once he became ill; this was just one example of the holy habits on which Bob had built his life. Keeping short accounts became one of my travel essentials.

A SURPRISE FEAST

One day, Bob came into the kitchen to tell me that there was a car in the driveway. At this point in the disease, he was seeing things that weren't there, so I kind of dismissed his announcement. I was busy preparing dinner and was frustrated with myself because I hadn't taken anything out of the freezer. *We'll just have a big salad with some hard-boiled eggs for added protein*, I thought.

But Bob pressed that it was a blue van and a woman had just gotten out. Somewhat frustrated, I looked out the door—to see a friend, Carolyn, walking up the driveway carrying several bags that I learned contained a dinner for us— pasta primavera, rolls, and dessert. She greeted us with a big smile and a huge apology. "I made dinner for you, but I didn't have time to make a salad!"

I needed to keep the house as simple as possible, to minimize David's confusion. We did not see many friends. I think they were uncomfortable with David's condition. I was on my own. Both our children were married and working full-time jobs.
—LORRAINE

I looked up in amazement, and with tears in my eyes, I shared that all I had for our dinner that night was a salad.

It was May 4; back in March, Carolyn had written in her calendar to bring us a meal on May 4. It was the earliest she could come because she had been out of town through late April! How God provides.

I was reminded of the Israelites traveling for forty years through the wilderness on their way to the Promised Land. They certainly had to travel light. In Exodus 16, we learn that God provided manna (bread wafers that tasted like honey) each day for them until they reached the border of Canaan. My manna that day had come in the form of a meal without a salad, reminding me that "my God will meet all [my] needs according to the riches of his glory in Christ Jesus" (Philippians 4:19).

Paula Spencer Scott, an Alzheimer's disease caregiving expert, highlights several essentials that every Alzheimer's caregiver needs.

> Most people simply dive in to the responsibility of caring for someone with Alzheimer's disease and then take it one day at a time. Fair enough. But before you find yourself combating both his disease and your own emotional strain and battle fatigue, be sure you have these stress-busters on your side.[9]

The following are three of her six essentials that I consider particularly important (comments are mine).

1. *Good self-care.* This is the easiest to forget, to dismiss. Bob's doctor kept reminding me of the importance of taking care of myself. Often, this would irritate me, as

I thought, *Isn't he Bob's doctor? Why is he so concerned about me?*

The challenges of caring for a loved one with Alzheimer's disease is that it is time-consuming, never-ending, and heart-wrenching. Caregiver burnout is real and comes in all shapes and sizes.

While different things work for different people, I found my escape in reading. Early on, Bob didn't have a problem sleeping (at least one of us slept through the night!). I had to go to bed when he did because my presence next to him gave him a sense of security. So, what to do with all that time? Read! I would read in bed for hours.

Bob loved to walk, so we would take a walk every day. It didn't give me time to myself, but at least I was getting exercise.

It's important not to get lost in the role of a caregiver. At first, I felt guilty about doing something for me. But I missed the stimulation of a good conversation and wanted to serve in some meaningful way beyond the role as caregiver. One day, a call came inviting me to consider serving on the governing board at our church. It would involve an evening meeting every two weeks. At first I thought, *Impossible*, but I couldn't get the idea out of my mind. *Maybe, just maybe, this might work.*

First, I talked with Bob's doctor. His response was "Accept! It will make you a better caregiver." Still not convinced, I asked a few friends if they would consider spending an evening with Bob while I attended these meetings. I would provide dinner, and they would provide companionship for Bob. To my surprise, most responded enthusiastically and insisted that they would provide dinner. Each person made it a point to tell me how privileged they felt to be part of caring and helping. Bob loved being with his friends and looked forward to those evenings. I loved having a break and returned refreshed.

My solutions may not work in your personal situation, but caring for yourself is a priority, and finding small ways to make this happen will prove life-changing. Trust God to help you find a way. Talk with a friend for some ideas. Be on the lookout for small opportunities to care for yourself.

2. *Realistic expectations.* When our journey began, I had no idea what a physical and emotional roller-coaster ride was ahead of us. My expectations, at first, were certainly unrealistic. I was not prepared for the changes we would meet as Bob's disease eroded more and more of his brain. Those lessons would be learned day by day.

You may find a support group to be a real source of strength and encouragement. I found encouragement and guidance from friends (new and old) who had been on this journey before me. I was also encouraged by accessing information online and having a good medical support system. I learned to let Bob lead the way, and this kept frustration (for him and me) to a minimum.

The time came when going to visit friends wasn't easy anymore, so short visits at our home became the norm. We used to love eating out, but even that had come to an end. Bathroom needs dictated the length of our walks and car rides. We had always looked forward to the time when we'd be the crazy grandparents cheering on our grandkids on the side of the soccer or baseball field, but whenever I tried attending a game with Bob, it always ended up in a struggle, a sense of panic, or a race to drive back to the safety of our own home.

Once I learned what parameters we were dealing with, I was able to abandon those unrealistic expectations and accept the reality of how this journey would ultimately end.

3. *A game plan.* A friend recently referred to her Alzheimer's journey as one of "human hopelessness." She is in the beginning stages of her husband's disease, and memories of my early days roll over me as I watch her taking each hesitant step into the uncertainty. *Human hopelessness* is an accurate description.

The diagnosis of Alzheimer's disease is the start of a slow process of deterioration, of getting worse day by day. What is lost will never be recovered. The disease is a thief that steals personality, memories, and connection. It's entering into a world that is seemingly out of control—at least, out of *your* control. One of the hardest tasks on this uncertain road is to link the practical with the emotional. While there is no guarantee regarding the time line of the disease, things can be done to make the emotional toll and transition a bit easier.

Even though the Israelites had no idea where the Promised Land was, nor when they would get there, God told them what they needed to bring (and not bring) as they started out. They were told to travel light.

For me, traveling light meant to focus only on what was needed and to trust God for His provision and faithfulness as we approached a sudden bend in the road.

The first thing I did, and each caregiver should do, is to address necessary changes regarding legal, medical, and financial areas. Don't be afraid to ask. Get it done. Then put the paperwork in an envelope and breathe easier that those important decisions are taken care of. While there will be rough roads ahead, you have a plan, and a huge part of the plan has been addressed.

> *The thing a caregiver needs the most is someone who will listen to and love on them, not try to "understand" and "fix things." Many people have great intentions, but unless you have lived being an Alzheimer's caregiver, there is no way you can really understand.*
> —KELLY

Scott continues, "It's one thing to understand the progression of the disease but a different matter to put a corresponding action plan in place. . . . Start talking with family members about these things now, even if they're difficult."[10]

A RAY OF HOPE

Human hopelessness. Yes, those are accurate words. But as our journey continued, I found much comfort in the chorus to the hymn "Great Is Thy Faithfulness":

Morning by morning new mercies I see.
All I have needed Thy hand hath provided—
Great is Thy faithfulness, Lord, unto me!

And so, I forged on. His mercies were new every morning (even a morning with an open freezer door), especially when I watched for them. Some habits, though, are hard to break. Some lessons are hard to learn. I still don't pack as well as I should, and I still get nervous when my luggage is weighed at the airport. But, for a season, my travel essentials were light and my God was, and continues to be, faithful.

Traveling Light

Don't weigh yourself down with if-onlys. Focus on self-care, adjust your expectations, and design a game plan to follow—even if only loosely. Trust in your faithful God.

A Prayer to Guide You

*God, when I am afraid, You usher me to safety and
prepare a place for me to rest my mind and spirit.
In the haven of Your care, Your calming presence
assures me that Your purpose prevails over my failings,
mistakes, and worries. Your love is my protection and
is a salve to my fears. It is my greatest blessing. Amen.*

HOPE LYDA, *Prayers to Soothe Your Soul*

CHAPTER 5

HOMESICK!

No longer forward nor behind
I look in hope or fear;
But, grateful, take the good I find,
The best of now and here.

JOHN GREENLEAF WHITTIER,
My Psalm: The Poetical Work in Four Volumes

HOME. The word conjures up all sorts of emotions and memories. The dictionary defines *home* as one's place of residence, a familiar setting, a place of origin. For me, home had always been a place where I could walk in, close the door, look around, and know everything's okay. It was a place of safety, a place of the familiar, a place to be me.

Both Bob and I grew up in Italian families. Our homes were loud, filled with food and people, with extended family always dropping in, and (for the most part) laughter, as extended family members shared memories of shared life.

The home we created was similar—a busy one. We

had three very active children who, with each passing year, seemed to add more activities to an already overloaded schedule. Our elderly neighbor laughingly shared that he loved to sit on his front steps and watch cars enter and exit our driveway. He said it became a game for him to guess how many kids occupied those cars that came and how many would leave in those very same cars—never the same number. And still, home was a place of safety, a place of the familiar, a place where I could take off my coat (and my mask) and just be me. It felt good.

CHANGE

I barely noticed at first. We were enjoying our empty nest, delighting in our grandchildren, and were happily very busy. On the outside, life looked like it hadn't changed, yet at the same time, it was completely different. A stranger had come to live in our familiar, comfortable lives. Bob became increasingly quiet, was less interested in going out, and had a hard time with word retrieval (how I regret those frustrating exchanges when I grew so impatient with him). And over time, the number of folks who used to drop by dwindled. The quiet seemed to create a sound of its own. I was lonely.

I was homesick.

And our house was changing. Our home had never truly been organized, but I always knew where everything was. Slowly, it was being rearranged to satisfy Bob's sense of orderliness. This meant pictures continually being placed on different walls; items that he deemed unnecessary tossed outside, hidden beside the garage, or put in the trash; and things that he deemed important hidden in the most bizarre places. After an argument with customer service people about an unpaid bill, I discovered it in a catalog on the floor of Bob's home office.

It got to the point where I was beginning to adjust to this new life: I took a flashlight to check the side of our garage every evening, looked in the trash barrels for treasures, and got used to the surprise of where paintings would be assigned.

Most painful, though, was when Bob packed up everything in his home office. There were boxes on the floor and his desk, the walls were bare, his bookshelves were empty, and the filing cabinet had been moved to the door. Trying to hide my surprise and confusion, I asked why he was packed up. Bob smiled and said, "I'm going home."

"Interesting," I responded. We had lived in our home for forty years. "Where is that?"

He told me he was going back to the town where he grew up and back to the home he owned there (Bob had never owned a home there).

"I'm not sure I want to move right now," I said.

He looked at me wide-eyed and said, "Oh, you're not coming with me. But you can visit anytime you want."

Wow, that response really pierced my heart. His office

> *I missed my time. Our entire lives revolved around Irene. Every invitation and opportunity brought the questions, "What will we do with Irene? What if something happens to her while we are away?" And she was in an assisted-living facility. We felt a tremendous responsibility to visit daily and to monitor her condition and needs closely.*
> —TERRY

remained packed up for the next two years. Ready to go. Alone.

THE THINGS I MISSED

I missed our rich *conversations*. We could talk for hours, challenging each other to think outside the box. We could solve any and every one of the world's problems. I admired his wisdom, his insights, and his ability to get to the heart of the matter—all matters. Conversation now centered around the weather, what we would have for lunch or dinner, the weather again, and his life experiences (all of which contained a kernel of truth).

I missed our *shared history*. As Alzheimer's disease continued its cruel progress, Bob's memories were on a sharp decline. It was becoming painfully clear that I was now the owner of our memories. We had been married for forty-seven years, had three children and five perfect grandchildren—yet Bob would ask me how we met, whether we were married, and how long we'd lived in our home (or, actually, how long had I been living in the home, since he thought he had been there long before I was).

Etched in my heart, even today, is the night when Bob was sitting in our family room and I went out to join him,

My life has been consumed by becoming Mom's caregiver. It's a full-time job: managing her doctor appointments and her medications, being her advocate, washing her feet, spending time with her. When I plan my week, I now schedule when I can squeeze in time to see her. I miss life without this heavy responsibility.
—VALERIE

and he looked at me and asked, "Do you know where my wife went?" With a smile (but with a broken heart) I said, "Oh, she went out to do some errands. She'll be back shortly." Bob returned the smile. Yet another Disney World choice: We were living in Bob's fantasy world. His world was intact; mine was shattering.

I was beginning to see this journey of ours more clearly. Our slow, sad trek persisted, but rather than traveling side by side, I was taking the lead. The ache of Bob giving up his beloved truck still dwelled in my heart. He no longer remembered, but I did. He was mostly happy; I carried the heartache alone. I kept asking, *Where is this journey taking us, when will it end, and how?*

Most of all, I missed *all that we were going to miss.* All the togethers we were supposed to share, to do together. Growing old together, reflecting on our many years together, lessons learned, mistakes made, seeing our future unfold through the lives of our grandchildren. But hardest, and perhaps saddest, of all is the fact that I don't even know what I missed.

> *Grow old along with me!*
> *The best is yet to be,*
> *the last of life, for which the first was made.*
> ROBERT BROWNING, "Rabbi Ben Ezra"

Our future was over. Alzheimer's robbed us of our future. There were no more memories to make together.

But in another sense, the best is still yet to be. While Alzheimer's disease shortened our time to grow old together, eternity now holds a new and personal significance. The words I spoke to the doctor on diagnosis day, "I'm going to live on the other side of eternity," were now becoming reality.

MARY AND MARTHA

> As Jesus and his disciples were on their way, he came to a village where a woman named Martha opened her home to him. She had a sister called Mary, who sat at the Lord's feet listening to what he said. But Martha was distracted by all the preparations that had to be made. She came to him and asked, "Lord, don't you care that my sister has left me to do the work by myself? Tell her to help me!"
>
> "Martha, Martha," the Lord answered, "you are worried and upset about many things, but few things are needed—or indeed only one. Mary has chosen what is better, and it will not be taken away from her."
>
> LUKE 10:38-42

Hospitality and home meant different things to Martha and Mary, even though they were important to both sisters. Martha expressed her hospitality and love of home by her busyness. Mary expressed her hospitality and love of home by her devoted attention to her houseguest. I began to see that I was more like Martha—always busy, always worried and focused as I tried to keep the ever-important schedule. And I took pride in being a multitasker, in checking things off my list, in breathing a sigh of relief when the day was over. I used to smugly say that no one would have had dinner if it were left up to Mary.

I slowly began to see this story through the eyes and heart of an Alzheimer's caregiver. Throughout his illness, Bob never acknowledged that he was anything but the healthiest man around. He savored the simple things. He wasn't interested in gourmet meals anymore. He didn't even care if the house was clean (whew, that was a relief). He just enjoyed my company.

Bob was content. He lived in the present. Yet he was heading home, and in some way, I believe he knew it.

A friend who walked with Bob weekly sent me an email recalling some memories of those walks. Her email is, for me, a window into Bob's soul, and I am grateful for this glimpse into the world of the one with whom I shared life. She wrote:

Of course we know "home is where the heart is." But my daughter gave me a plaque when I moved that said "Home is where your mom is" and that was, and is, a treasure to me. In that vein, for Bob, home was where Cynthia was.

We would be walking home and Bob would say, "Where is Cynthia?" If we were at the house and you were not there, he would ask, "Where is Cynthia?" again. . . .

His home was safe with you there. It was his place of love, trust, safety, and comfort.

He knew the way home even when the days of much recognition were mostly gone. "Here," he would remind me, "take this corner, we are in Bobville!"

I remember going the long way home to give you
a bit more time, and he knew I went the different
way and did not like that. He wanted his home
when he was ready to be there.

It was where he was safe with you.

A few times I was invited to sit in the backyard,
even when you were home. All was well then.

It is interesting to think about how God was
preparing Bob for another home, in a sort of way.
Remember how Bob was packing to move to Quincy
[the town where he grew up], and that was before
you were actually thinking he may have to move
to a safe environment? He was in a sense preparing
for change before you were ready. And, Cynthia,
that must have hurt, in a way that would be hard to
explain to anyone.

In that place of Quincy there were many people
that he loved, places that were nostalgic for him, and
a home where he grew up. Was that a sort of forecast
of heaven for him?

Home at this time, as I see it, was a mix of
joy, peace, love, confusion, and agitation for him,
probably for you, too. It was a privilege to be a part
of Bob's walk to and from home!

AMBIGUOUS GRIEF

> *Everybody needs his memories. They keep the*
> *wolf of insignificance from the door.*

SAUL BELLOW, *Mr. Sammler's Planet*

Esther Heerema offers helpful advice about the grief we feel when confronted with our loved one's loss of memory.

> In its early stages, Alzheimer's disease typically affects short-term memory. . . . However, as the disease progresses, people gradually experience more long-term memory loss. . . .
>
> People with Alzheimer's may have difficulty finding words; memories of significant events, such as weddings, may fade; and anything that requires multiple steps might become lost.
>
> For example, family members often appear familiar to those with advancing dementia, but they might not be able to identify the specific relationship. In the late stages of Alzheimer's, your loved one might not be able to demonstrate an awareness of your presence. . . .
>
> Remember that the loss of a special memory, or even who you are, is not an indicator that you aren't meaningful or special to that person. It's a result of the disease, not a choice that he is making.
>
> Don't constantly remind the person of her memory loss. Love her unconditionally and be with her.[11]

Trying to keep that wolf of insignificance away from Bob's door was my goal. To make our home a place where Bob would feel secure and safe was my heart's desire. It was a painful realization—to acknowledge that life would never be the same, that while we were on this journey together, our destinations were different. I was reminded of the two goals I had set for this journey: to preserve Bob's dignity and to preserve my sanity. I think that sums it up.

Those years were my season of ambiguous grief—grieving the loss of someone who is still alive. Bob was still with me, but he was becoming someone I didn't know. And he no longer knew who I was. If asked, Bob would often say that I was the lady who lived in his house and was kind to him. That was okay with me. He looked the same . . . except for that vacant stare, which we caregivers know so well. But he acted differently. We no longer shared life and responsibilities like we used to, and there were even times when he said things that were strange and sometimes hurtful. We were living as a couple, but I was living alone, grieving for what I (we) had lost.

Alzheimer's has taken my dad—and my mom—from me (and my family). His caregiver at home for eight years, Mom is now very much in the trenches with his care at the memory-care facility . . . My kids don't have grandparents who come to their events. They don't go to Nana and Papa's house for a sleepover.

*—*Hope

It happened in an instant. I was walking through the dining room to go check on Bob. Like a flash of lightning, the clarity exploded before me. We were moving in opposite directions. Bob was on a journey out of his fog to where his faith would become sight. But I was moving into deeper fog, one that obscured all that was familiar to me, all that made up the security in my life: home, Bob, family. Once again, I was at a crossroads. I had to make yet another choice: Would I live bemoaning all that I had missed, or would I live trusting that God would care for my needs, for our tomorrows, and for today?

I learned the language of ambiguous grief from the website whatsyourgrief.com. While the article "Ambiguous Grief: Grieving Someone Who Is Still Alive" wasn't written until after Bob's death, it did give me a name for my homesickness. The author suggests five ways to cope with ambiguous grief:

1. Remember that the present doesn't override the past.
2. Understand that the illness isn't the person.
3. Acknowledge the grief and pain of the loss.
4. Be open to a new type of relationship.
5. Connect with others who can relate.[12]

TOUCHES OF GRACE

Increasingly, Bob would say, "God is taking care of me." As I look back, I see his words as a reminder for me, almost like a love letter with some instructions that he was leaving for me. I clung to the hope that God was, and is, taking care of me as well—while on our Alzheimer's journey in the here and now and in the moments to come.

Watch for God's touches of grace—reminders that He is taking care of you and your loved one, even when things are the darkest.

What a strange journey. What a cruel disease. It robbed us of *us*. I was homesick for what used to be us, and I knew that *us* would never be again. Sure, there were all sorts of guidelines, suggestions, dos and don'ts. But one quote—a March 1, 2016, tweet from John Piper—just resonated in my heart, gave validity to what I was feeling, authenticated the ambiguous grief, and pointed me to God, who knew my hurt and who hurt for me also:

Occasionally weep deeply over the life you hoped would be. Grieve the losses. Then wash your face. Trust God. And embrace the life you have.

And so, our journey continued.

Traveling Light

Homesickness can blind us: It causes us to focus on what we've lost. But as caregivers, we need to live in the moment and savor the scenery, because we'll pass this way only once.

A Prayer to Guide You

Dear God, I spend so much time reliving yesterday or anticipating tomorrow that I lose sight of the only time that is really mine, the present moment. You give today one moment at a time. That's all I have, all I ever will have. Give the faith which knows that each moment contains exactly what is best for me. Give the hope which trusts You enough to forget past failings and future trials. Give the love which makes each moment an anticipation of eternity with You. We ask this in the name of Jesus Who is the same yesterday, today and forever. Amen.

COLUMBAN.ORG, *Daily Prayer—One Moment at a Time*

CHAPTER 6

SUSTENANCE ALONG THE WAY

Let nothing disturb you,
Let nothing frighten you,
All things are passing away:
God never changes.
Patience obtains all things.
Whoever has God lacks nothing;
God alone suffices.

ST. TERESA OF AVILA

IT WAS AS IF we were moving further and further away from home and all I knew to be familiar and comforting. The view was often clouded with sadness and storm clouds. Bob seemed content and blissful in his own corner of the world, yet he was becoming increasingly distant and insecure. For a while, during breakfast, I would read from a simple devotional and he would listen—no response except for a smile now and again. Over time, he began interrupting me, to ask what we were going to do that day or occasionally to just get up and leave the room. Our devotional time became shorter—eventually, just my quick prayer for us each morning. Even the quick prayer became nonexistent after a while. Bob was full, both from a good breakfast and the knowledge that I was with him. I was empty, missing all those things that filled my life with meaning and joy: a thriving relationship with my husband; the freedom to come and go as I pleased; some alone time to think, to read, and to ponder God's Word. And how I missed my weekly Bible study that had enriched me spiritually.

My faith was essential, knowing that the final timing of Mom's life was in God's hands, not mine. Toward the end, God and I had many conversations about His timing. Mom was a woman of faith, and I struggled to understand why God didn't take her home and relieve her suffering.

—DONNA

Early in our journey, our pastor encouraged our congregation to gather in small groups through Lent. I was quietly excited and asked Bob if he'd like to have some people in for lunch and Bible study. He seemed interested. I made a list of some folks that he knew and read the names to him (his reading skills had diminished by this time). Bob selected a wonderful group of people who became a special part of our lives. We began meeting weekly. However, as time passed, Bob would get up and wander through the house or sit out in the back yard, and he needed encouragement to join us for lunch.

My life had so radically changed—once so involved in so much, I now felt that I had been bumped from the game and was sitting on the sidelines watching everyone else with their assigned positions, playing at the life they had been given. How I longed for the good old days. Are you missing the good old days? Every caregiver does.

EMBARRASSED

One day, while glancing through the Bible in the brief time I had available, I came to the story of the Samaritan woman. As I read this story, so familiar to me, the words became personal and the perspective new.

> Now he [Jesus] had to go through Samaria. . . . Jacob's well was there, and Jesus, tired as he was from the journey, sat down by the well. It was about noon.
>
> When a Samaritan woman came to draw water, Jesus said to her, "Will you give me a drink?" . . .
>
> The Samaritan woman said to him, "You are a Jew and I am a Samaritan woman. How can you ask me for a drink?" (For Jews do not associate with Samaritans.)
>
> Jesus answered her, "If you knew the gift of God and who it is that asks you for a drink, you would have asked him and he would have given you living water."
>
> "Sir," the woman said, "you have nothing to draw with and the well is deep. Where can you get this living water?" . . .
>
> Jesus answered, "Everyone who drinks this water will be thirsty again, but whoever drinks the water I give them will never thirst. Indeed, the water I give

them will become in them a spring of water welling up to eternal life."

The woman said to him, "Sir, give me this water so that I won't get thirsty and have to keep coming here to draw water."

JOHN 4:4-15

I stood there, holding my Bible, stunned. I was the Samaritan woman. I bowed my head and wept as I thought through my recent life. The man I was married to was not the man I married. For so many years, Bob was strong, wise, the one I leaned on for security. He was fun to be around. And now he was insecure, quiet, though still very kind. Did other people notice this? Did people talk about us?

Like the Samaritan woman, I would plan errands around times when the fewest people would be around. She went to draw water at noon—the hottest time of the day—because no one else would be there. Bob and I would go grocery shopping when I thought there would be the fewest customers. What if someone I knew saw me, saw Bob? What if they asked him a question and his response had nothing to do with the question? What if I saw some people I knew, and they went the other way? Of course, they must be trying to avoid us.

Over time I came to realize that I could not carry a grudge against the people who didn't understand, or who

> *If I didn't have a close relationship with the Lord, I wouldn't be able to do this part of life's journey—but that was also true before Alzheimer's.*
>
> —JAN

ignored us, or who said the wrong things. First, they probably didn't do it on purpose or to hurt me. Second, a grudge
is too heavy a burden to drag along with me through life.

Except for our little Bible-study group, our circle
became very small and we became increasingly isolated.
Until that day when I went to the "well" (God's Word) and
met myself, the Samaritan woman.

> The Samaritan woman grasped what He said with a
> fervor that came from an awareness of her real need.
>
> The transaction was fascinating. She had come
> with a bucket. He sent her back with a spring of
> living water.
>
> She had come as a reject. He sent her back being
> accepted by God Himself.
>
> She came wounded. He sent her back whole.
>
> She came laden with questions. He sent her back
> as a source for answers.
>
> She came living a life of quiet desperation. She
> ran back overflowing with hope.
>
> The disciples missed it all. It was lunchtime for
> them.[13]

I thought back to that diagnosis day in the doctor's
office, when our lives took a turn down a one-way street. I
remembered feeling numb, seemingly wrapped in a blanket
of fog, yet "hearing" God speak to my heart: "I'm here, and
I will restore whatever years the locusts will have eaten."
Back then, the doctor's voice broke into the fog, and I
remembered as he asked, "Cynthia, how are you going to

handle this?" Without a moment's hesitation, I responded, "I'm going to live on the other side of eternity." Yet here I was, living with a soul that was drying up, thirsty for His living water. How, in the midst of what was becoming a small and parched life, would I quench my thirsty soul?

SHRIVELED SOUL SYNDROME

When I originally planned this chapter, I expected to write about all the people who broke into our difficult world and became "Team Bob." As important as they were (and I will talk about them in another chapter), they could not fill my thirsty soul. I was lowering my bucket into the well and coming up empty. God alone, His living water, had to be my sustenance.

Paul Borthwick has written an article "10 Ways for Avoiding 'Shriveled Soul Syndrome.'" With his permission, I have adapted some of his guidelines that I feel are helpful for Alzheimer's caregivers:

1. *Avoid gossip.* "Gossip shrinks our souls by diminishing our self-worth because we are living at the expense of others. We build our identity by tearing others down." (Time became a precious commodity for me, and I learned that I didn't have time to talk about others or listen to hearsay. This, in its own way, became freeing, although it did enlighten me about how easily we gossip under the guise of "we really should pray for . . .")

2. *Release bitterness.* "Bitter people shrivel spiritually as they walk through life under the weight of 'apologies

owed me.'" I soon learned that the majority of people don't understand what life with an Alzheimer's loved one is like. When they would say things that hurt, when we were excluded from certain gatherings, at first, I just wanted to scream, "Do you even get what I am going through?" But later, I began to realize that they didn't understand. And even with those who did understand but continued hurtful behavior, I had to move on—for the sake of my own soul.

3. *Take risks.* "Expanded souls step out in faith. Shriveled souls run when no one is pursuing. . . . [T]hey choose to live in fear of what might happen." One lovely spring day, I told Bob we were going on an adventure. I was nervous,

It's a progressive disease, so I never thought it would get better. Mom always smiled and was happy to see me, even though she didn't know who I was.
—DARLENE

but I had done all my homework, and off to Maine we went for the day. I had contacted a friend who had a beach home in York, Maine. "Can we use your home as our base—for bathroom needs (this was an increasingly difficult challenge) and just to leave some stuff?" "Of course," she responded. "I was hoping to figure out how to help you."

A couple of long walks on the beach (interrupted by several trips to the bathroom), some fun photos taken, lunch at our favorite restaurant (they remembered Bob), and memories that are carved into my heart and soul forever. God went before us and blessed us with a treasured day, and I will always be grateful.

4. *Trust.* "Living a life of worry guarantees a shrinking soul. . . . Enlarged souls live comfortably with the unknown because they choose to trust God." For every question posed to me about plans, my slogan became "I am like one of the Israelites. I'm standing at the Jordan River waiting for God to tell me when and where to cross." And He always did.

5. *Don't live for "stuff."* Living for the accumulation of things causes degeneration in our souls. I learned a lot from Bob about "stuff" as his world became very uncluttered: Visits from the grandkids, walks with friends, daily ice-cream treats, and his backyard chair gave him contentment and joy. Clutter is confusing; simplicity is desirable.

6. *Grow deep.* "Enlarged souls think about the meaning of life. They look for purpose. . . . Shriveled souls get preoccupied with drivel. . . . [T]hey find their conversations filled with superficiality." Alzheimer's disease has a way of filtering out this drivel and leaving room for the necessary. For the caregiver, the necessary includes caring for your loved one and yourself. Drinking deeply from His well of living water gave me direction and purpose: This is a season, God is with me and He cares, and direction will come when I need it. For the married caregiver, these are the "poorer," "sickness," and "worse" vows that we made to one another.[14]

While nothing makes the Alzheimer's journey easy, there is purpose and there are gifts to be discovered along the way. Look for them. In time you, too, will discover them. The prophet Isaiah reminds us of God's sustenance and His promises:

> I will give you hidden treasures,
>   riches stored in secret places,
> so that you may know that I am the LORD.

ISAIAH 45:3

Traveling Light

Caregiver stress is real. Jesus offered the Samaritan woman water that would quench her thirst forever. He offers you the same. Drink from His water and be refreshed.

A Prayer to Guide You

*Most loving Father, whose will it is for us to give
thanks for all things, to fear nothing but the loss of
you, and to cast all our care on you who cares for us:
Preserve me from faithless fears and worldly anxieties,
that no clouds of this mortal life may hide from me
the light of that love which is immortal, and which
you have manifested to us in your Son Jesus Christ our
Lord; who lives and reigns with you, in the unity of
the Holy Spirit, one God, now and for ever. Amen.*

THE BOOK OF COMMON PRAYER

CHAPTER 7

STORM CLOUDS GATHER

*The disappointment has come, precious child of
God, not because God desires to hurt you or make
you miserable or to demoralize you or ruin your life
or keep you from ever knowing happiness. Rather,
it comes because He wants you to be perfect and
complete in every aspect, lacking nothing . . . .
It's not the easy times that make you
more like Jesus but the hard times.*

KAY ARTHUR, *As Silver Refined*

I DID NOT JOURNAL or keep a diary during the years of
Bob's illness. Partly because I didn't want to remember
all the grisly details of our sojourn through Alzheimer's
disease, but mostly because I just didn't have the time or
energy. Most days started early and ended late. Over time,
Bob didn't seem to require much sleep, and I needed to
be alert during his daytime waking hours and even the
few short hours he slept each night. Consequently, I was
exhausted.

In the second year of his illness, I managed to read a very short devotional book, *Jesus Calling*. I would write a phrase or two in response to each entry—sometimes a word, sometimes a plea to the Lord, always brief.

In the year following Bob's death, I retrieved that devotional and added it to my quiet-time reading. Seeing my comments written over two years previous, I was struck by the depth of my journey, the sadness in those cavernous valleys, and my total and utter dependence on Him, the navigator of my journey. Here are some of the things I wrote:

- Yes, You are speaking directly to me! (The author had written, "I am leading you, step by step, through your life. Hold My hand, in trusting dependence.")
- I need to learn this. (The author had written, "Though you lose everything else, if you gain My peace you are rich indeed.")
- I'm trying, Lord, but it's been a very hard day. I am so sad and confused. I need clear directions and hope.
- I do feel so alone.
- Sometimes the pain/hurt runs deeper than words, Lord. The cruelty of a friend is beyond comprehension.
- Thank You for your presence. Handle this mess or show me how, because I have no idea.
- I am so weary. I don't think I can do this, Lord.

A line from Skye Jethani's book *Singing at Midnight* described me well: "There is a sorrow words cannot express and no embrace can remove. It abides deep within, and is accessible only to the one who carries it."[15] I used to jokingly say, "I'm treading water and am okay until the next wave hits." And hit they did.

Alzheimer's disease is so unpredictable. It is not a gradual decline. More often than not, it is a drop, then a plateau, then another drop, determined by which parts of the brain the disease is attacking. For me, each plateau brought new turbulence, thicker and darker clouds, increasing winds, and the realization that we would never return to what once was. This journey was becoming more complicated.

I began to understand that I didn't live in Kansas anymore. But, unlike Dorothy in *The Wizard of Oz*, I had no magic red slippers that could return me to my Kansas—the life I knew. Everything in my life had changed, and if I was going to survive, I needed to roll with the changes. People of faith know that although we have the confidence of the anticipation of heaven, our earthly story won't always have a happy ending. And I needed to come to grips with that.

GRILLED CHEESE

Bob used to love grilled cheese sandwiches. One day, he couldn't figure out how to eat one and just kept picking it up, looking it over, and setting it down.

I said, "Oops, I forgot to cut it." What was the point of asking him why he was having a problem? I cut it into quarters; he was thrilled and ate it easily.

A few weeks later, the sandwich quarters had to be cut

into smaller, bite-size pieces. Soon, he began eating all his food with his fingers, having forgotten what his fork was for.

One day, Bob could do something on his own. The next day, he couldn't—good-bye. The next week, something else was forgotten—good-bye.

> *I get aggravated and annoyed, and my husband reminds me that this is par for the course with this disease. Mom used to be so proud of herself for doing laundry, but now she's regressed to not doing it at all. So we talk, one more time, about how it's necessary to change underwear and socks daily.*
> —VALERIE

Good-byes are always sad. Perhaps you are experiencing the sad good-byes that Alzheimer's offers. Whether these are huge good-byes like not being able to drive anymore or small good-byes like not remembering how to eat a sandwich, they are still good-byes, and they are still sad. How I wish I could share with you a secret formula to alleviate the pain you, as a caregiver, are experiencing. There is no secret formula.

But I can tell you two things. First, you are not alone. A whole cadre of other caregivers are experiencing the same sadness you are experiencing.

Second, God understands. He knows your hurt heart. That is one of the rays of His lingering light that hovered over me during our journey.

LESSONS FROM JOSEPH

When our kids were young, our family became *Joseph and the Amazing Technicolor Dreamcoat* groupies. I think we saw the musical five or six times. We knew the words to every song, and it became tradition to dance and sing to the music each Christmas Eve. Even my eighty-year-old dad joined in the festivities. Through the years, I viewed this musical through eyes that reflected the seasons of life our kids were in.

I was sad when Joseph's brothers turned on him in jealousy, and I prayed that our children would always view each other with love and respect.

I prayed that our teenage children would make good decisions when faced with "Mrs. Potiphar" choices and would run from evil, whatever the consequences.

And I prayed that as adult children, they would live a life of freedom and forgiveness when face-to-face with those who intended to hurt them.

All those years I prayed for our children, I had no idea that these Joseph lessons would be intended for me one day.

Probably the saddest experience for me was when friends didn't understand the disease. They didn't know how isolating it was and how it affected everything we did and how we interacted with others. I needed help (more in the next chapter), and Bob needed social interaction at the level that worked for him.

Bob needed to see other people, other friends. But he wasn't able to make plans. If he agreed to meet his friend Fred for lunch on Thursday, he would immediately forget both the date and the friend, so that when Fred arrived on Thursday, Bob might not even be at home.

Sadly, some friends didn't understand why we needed all plans to be made through me. Over time, the phone stopped ringing, and our world was reduced to a small circle of friends, with some cavernous holes left by those who had walked away.

The more I talked with people in my situation, the more I learned that this is common. I heard the same sentence from so many: "Alzheimer's disease destroyed my family, and I lost many friends."

I prayed Joseph prayers for myself—that I would:

- forgive family members and friends who did not understand,
- continue to treat Bob with love and respect, protecting his dignity, and
- make good decisions when faced with a "Mrs. Potiphar" choice.

A Bible verse is now taped to the corner of my computer:

> Make every effort to live in peace with everyone and to be holy; without holiness no one will see the Lord. See to it that no one falls short of the grace of God and that no bitter root grows up to cause trouble and defile many.
>
> HEBREWS 12:14-15

I kept trying to extend grace even though my heart was breaking.

DECISION TIME

Medications were always changing. Some worked for a while; others never worked. Some had negative effects and had to be adjusted or eliminated. These were difficult decisions and best discussed in detail with our doctor.

Medical procedures were another challenge—to proceed or not to proceed? There were always several options. With guidance from our doctor (along with my daughter, who is in the medical field), I examined the value of each procedure, and we made decisions that we felt were best for Bob and his failing health.

When it became clear that Bob needed more socialization (and I needed a break), I visited an adult day-care center. It was wonderful. The staff were so friendly, there were lots of activities, and Bob would be there twice a week for eight hours a day. They even provided drop-off and pickup services. I was giddy with excitement and began planning all the things I would do in those precious sixteen hours a week.

I was surprised and hurt by the lack of support from friends and our church. As the disease progressed, I felt abandoned by all but a few. No one visited, offered to help, or checked in to see how I was doing. Society does not comprehend the enormous emotional and financial toll this disease takes on patients and their families.

—SARAH

Bob came with me for the next visit, and I was so looking forward to showing him this amazing place. He was very quiet, very polite, but I could see his eyes darting to every person and every corner of the rooms. When we got home, he put his hands on his hips, looked at me, and said, "I will never go to a place like that."

My plans dissolved; my dreams were shattered. I was angry. Then I looked into his eyes and saw something I had never seen before: fear.

Someone once said that the eyes are the windows to the heart and soul. And Bob's heart and soul were trembling—he didn't know these people, I wouldn't be with him, and it was more than he could bear.

Decision time—and I had to make it alone.

This is what the LORD says:

"Stand at the crossroads and look;
      ask for the ancient paths,
ask where the good way is, and walk in it,
      and you will find rest for your
            souls."

JEREMIAH 6:16

You might be struggling with a difficult decision and find that you have to make it alone. The answer is different for everyone. Ask God where the good way is, what the right path is, and then follow it. Doing so will give you peace—rest for your soul.

Bob never went to adult day care. But God opened up another way. I learned from a friend that a woman named Judy was starting a home-care business. I called her, and she was delighted to have Bob as her first client. She agreed to come to our home once a week to hang out with Bob so I could leave.

Bob was happy to have a visitor, but as I pulled out of our driveway that first day, I felt like I was leaving my child at the door of the kindergarten room. I was in tears, so concerned about how he would do while I was gone.

Not only that, but where would I go? I had no plan. I had packed my lunch, so I drove to a parking lot, ate lunch . . . and sobbed.

Eventually, we settled into a rhythm. Bob looked forward to his friend Judy and another friend, Eileen (when I added another day), coming to visit him, going for walks, eating lunch, and enjoying a few simple adventures together. In the beginning, I went to our son's home and sat on their back patio. I then asked if I could use a room at our church. I savored the quiet, working on fleece blankets for Christmas gifts, reading a book, or sometimes just looking out the window. This went on for a year or so, and because Bob seemed to be at peace, I was also.

CHURCH

One of the most difficult decisions came when it became clear that Bob could no longer attend church. How he loved going to church—to worship, to teach a class for seekers, to greet newcomers, to visit with his pals. But now, bathroom issues, a decreasing attention span, and a growing restlessness were among the problems we faced.

Fortunately, our church offers livestreaming, so we were able to sit at home and watch the service. My biggest concerns were that Bob would miss seeing his friends and worshiping with others. If there is a sweetness to Alzheimer's, it is this: Bob could live contentedly in the present, unaware of what he was missing. It was a lesson I needed to learn.

Those Sunday mornings were some of the most precious times we spent together. I will always treasure the memory of singing along with Bob as the words to the hymns were shown on the screen. It soon became painfully apparent that he wasn't able to read the words, but he could still sing because, over many years of following Christ, those lyrics had been engraved on his heart.

Did I always make the right decisions? Of course not. There were some real blunders, believe me. Some outbursts that should never have happened, some anger that I held deep inside, some regrets over words that spilled out before I could hold them back. But, to this day, I trust that God knew my heart and understood my frailty. My comfort comes in knowing that Bob, because of Alzheimer's, did not remember what happened on any particular day, and he taught me to keep short accounts.

Like Joseph, caregivers need to understand that we don't own this journey, that we don't know (nor do we need to know) the plans God has for us. What we do need to know, and embrace, is that He is guiding us every step of the way. Sometimes this means that our head has to rule over our heart. And we caregivers need to be kind to ourselves. The storm will clear—when and how, we don't know, but it will clear—and there will be beautiful moments of sunshine.

Traveling Light

Storms come. Storms pass. Trust our faithful God, and you will get "there" eventually.

A Prayer to Guide You

Gracious Lord, once again, I see the dark clouds approaching and feel the wind beginning to swirl around me. I want to run for cover, hide from the approaching storm. Your Word reminds me to be still. It says You will lead me to still waters even in the midst of the storm. I know that when the waves are raging, the deeper I go, the more still the water becomes. Draw me deeper, Lord. Lead me to those still waters, that I may rest in You. Thank You for being my shelter in past storms; I want to trust You for this storm and the storms that I know are ahead. And so I run to You for cover, I hide in the shelter of Your wings, and I bask in Your powerful and peace-filled love for me.

CYNTHIA FANTASIA

CHAPTER 8

IT TAKES A VILLAGE

Sometimes we need someone to simply be there . . .
not to fix anything or do anything in particular, but
just to let us feel we are supported and cared about.

UNKNOWN

THE HOUSE WAS eerily quiet. Her car was in the driveway, but they were nowhere to be found. I wandered through each room, my footsteps echoing on the hardwood floors. A half-eaten apple and a banana peel in the kitchen sink—normal. I called out Bob's name. No answer.

She would have called me on my cell if there had been a problem, so I wasn't too concerned. But still! It was a beautiful spring day. Maybe they went out for a walk? I peered out the living-room window and strained my eyes looking up and down the street. Nothing!

Then I heard laughter from somewhere in the distance. Racing over to the dining-room window, I spotted them. Bob and Eileen were sitting under a tree in the far corner of our backyard, happily chatting away. Eileen visited (that's how we explained it to Bob) once a week for five hours, giving me time to do errands, schedule doctor's appointments, or meet up with a friend or two. Basically, Eileen gave me a window of freedom to keep up with my life.

FAMILY

In the beginning, I had grandiose expectations that I would be able to care for Bob for as long as he lived. That was in the beginning. Alzheimer's disease has a way of creeping up on a caregiver, catching you off guard, and sapping your strength ever so slowly. Yet the Alzheimer's patient moves on through life seemingly unaware of the regression in his/her body and mind. Bob remained happy—eating breakfast while watching the cars drive by our home, spending four happy hours "trimming" the shrubs in our backyard, one inch at a time (often right to the ground), asking the same questions every fifteen minutes or so, and occasionally (but with increasing regularity) plugging the drains and stuffing the toilets. (I jokingly told people that I had the plumber on speed dial.)

I became pretty good at the role of detective, finder of lost or hidden things. I would ask myself, *Where is the* least *likely place that object would be?* Sometimes it was obvious: All his socks were dumped in the bathtub. Sometimes it was more difficult: I found the banana peels inside the window seat only by following their scent. Reprimands were useless, because by this time, Bob had already forgotten he had eaten the banana, much less secured a safe place for its peel. Meanwhile, as I was searching, Bob would invent another "creative" activity.

Most days, it was just the two of us, except for surprise visits from our grandkids on their way home from school. Sometimes those visits would be the result of an SOS text to their mom. Their car would pull into the driveway, and after a short toot of the horn, three little ones would tumble out of the car, running up the driveway, arms open wide, calling for BobBob. It was instantaneous joy on Bob's face as they wrapped themselves around his arms and legs.

Family played an important role in our lives. We were fortunate to have family close by, familiar faces who would drop by just to hang with their dad and their BobBob. Family I could be honest with—to a point. I had to learn to be honest with them. At first, I didn't want to burden them, to alter their lives and busy schedules, to worry them. But they lovingly persisted and understood without me saying too much. I am so grateful for their mature, supportive, caring ways.

One big mistake many caregivers make is trying to shelter our families from the cruel realities of this disease. We overprotect because, after all, we are the parents. We often bear the whole burden of caring for a spouse who is becoming increasingly weak and troublesome. But this overprotection denies our children a chance to take care of both the ill parent and the exhausted caregiver. And if the caregiving parent becomes unable to continue and has not explained how to navigate their spouse's care, the adult children are not prepared to pick up the mantle.

For me, it was difficult to begin sharing with my children the truth about their dad. Of course they knew about the disease, but they weren't aware of how exhausting life had become. But when I reached the point where I couldn't shoulder all the responsibilities on my own, their response was amazing. I looked at them with awe—they were adults (when did this happen?). And they joined with me as we made hard decisions.

This isn't always the case; some people live a distance from family and loved ones, have strained relationships with them, or are unwilling to address the reality of their loved one having Alzheimer's. If you don't have a family support system, ask God for one or two folks you can trust who already are or will become like family.

FRIENDS

Alzheimer's is a strange disease. Most people don't understand it and don't know what to say, so they stay away. Like meeting someone who only speaks a foreign language, people talk louder to someone with Alzheimer's. Many just pretend the person isn't present in a group setting or a conversation. I was grateful, at these times, for Bob's memory loss because he forgot those who never showed up or ignored him. But I bore the pain of their disappearance—for both of us.

Bob loved people, and he loved people who loved him. Like a small child who senses an adult's pleasure or displeasure with them, I could tell from Bob's body language whether he felt comfortable with an individual. He would smile and become animated when he felt accepted and loved yet would stiffen and draw back from those who just tolerated him. For you, my partners in caregiving, watch the body language, climb into your loved one's world, and protect them from anyone who creates a difficult atmosphere. Your loved one's world, in this season, is dependent on you providing security, safety, and love.

Our journey had been fairly peaceful thus far. But the loneliness of a world that was steadily shrinking made me very vulnerable. I just couldn't pick up the phone and ask for help. The fear of being turned down was more gripping than the weariness of the daily stress and sadness of our world. I thanked God every day that Bob didn't seem to be affected. But Bob always enjoyed being around people. He needed more than just TV and me. It was time to make some changes.

Even though he didn't remember them, Bob found comfort in the rhythm of routines. Early on, our friend Beth would visit Bob weekly, and they would go for a walk. They would walk to our town's center, stop at Starbucks, and enjoy coffee and lemon pound cake. Always the same. A long walk back home, sometimes a different route, but always the same topics of conversation: all the people Bob knew, where he grew up and how he was going to go back there soon, and the grandkids—oh, how he loved the grandkids!

Beth knew how vulnerable I felt. She saw that I was fearful about being rejected. One day, she leveled with me.

"You need more people. Bob loves to walk and talk, and you need a break—more than just twice a week. Why don't you give a few people a call and ask them to come on a certain day?" It must have been the blank look on my face that prompted her response: "Would you like me to get a team together?"

Thus, Team Bob began. Beth recruited two women who alternated walking with Bob on Thursdays for about an hour and a half. As the disease progressed, the walks shortened, and sometimes sitting in the backyard was the activity for that Thursday.

Bill, a longtime friend of Bob's, would come every other Wednesday. They would walk to the center, have lunch at a local pizza shop, and walk home. How Bob loved these walks and lunches—of course, he talked with every "friend" he met along the way, explained life to Bill, and returned home happy and full.

It's important to let people help—or ask people to help you. If you have even one friend, ask him or her to ask a few others to help out. Help is often just a phone call away. Not everyone can find a team of fifteen, but even a team of three or four is good. Make it clear: no experience necessary, flexible time commitment, no strenuous lifting.

You may find someone in your office, church, or book club who says, "I wish I could help." Take them up on it.

> *My husband fell out of bed. I struggled to pick him up. Minutes later, he fell out of bed again. I was frantic. I have a hard time asking for help, but I called a pastor friend, and he came over with his son. We took my husband to the hospital. Little did I know that he would never return home.*
>
> —LIZ

Call your local senior center or Council on Aging to discover what programs would be of interest to your loved one, and invite friends to share those programs with your loved one.

PROFESSIONAL CAREGIVERS

While Bob was enjoying his outings, I enjoyed the short respite of a quiet home. However, that "quiet time" usually included working through the never-ending piles of laundry. It also included taking care of bills, because if I tried to do this while Bob was home, he couldn't understand why he shouldn't take care of them as he used to. (Checks with no signature or the incorrect amount just didn't work.) This was also the time I could do housecleaning or handle any other task that had gone neglected. Yes, Bob returned home happy for having been on an adventure, but he was often greeted by a frazzled wife who had not completed the myriad of tasks she had on her list.

And then Bob began to refuse to leave our home. As his world was shrinking, home was becoming his world of security, safety, and familiarity. That's when we began bringing in professional help for extended periods of time. I didn't want to do this at first, because I felt it meant that I had failed as a caregiver. I wrestled with feelings of inadequacy.

Instead, I argued with myself about how I could do things differently, rationalized that we had married "for better or worse, in sickness and in health." And yet, in the "worse" and "sickness" areas, I wasn't measuring up. I lost every argument. I was doing my best, but it was more than one person could handle.

There are many resources available, and I encourage each caregiver to take advantage of as many as possible. For us, I wanted someone Bob was familiar with (although his memory was on a steady decline) and someone I could trust. Oh, how that trust factor tugged at my mind and heart!

I did quite a bit of reading, and this was helpful in answering many of my questions. I also kept careful notes on David's daily life. Three years after the diagnosis, I joined a support group. There, I found direction from others on the same road.

—LORRAINE

This was when Judy and Eileen entered our lives, each for five hours at a time—Judy on Tuesdays and Eileen on Fridays. Bob enjoyed the walks, puzzles, projects, conversation, sharing about family, and deep friendship that filled these hours for him.

I keep revisiting that first day when I backed out of the driveway, leaving Bob with Judy. Is this how Jochebed felt when she put her precious son, Moses, in a straw basket and slipped it gently into the Nile? Did her heart ache like mine? Did she doubt, even a little, that God had Moses' best in mind? How long did Moses' sister keep a distant watch over her brother (Exodus 2:1-10)? I won't tell you how many times I drove by our home that first day—just to make sure everything was all right.

But that initial anxiety settled, and for this portion of our journey, we were good. Bob had his team, and I had my little hidden sanctuary. Enjoying the company of his friends (he had no inkling they were anything else), Bob would say gratefully over and over to me: "God is so good.

All these friends want to spend time with me." He seemed content, my batteries were recharged, and while the future remained uncertain, we could both enjoy this season—for whatever time God allowed.

> *Said a wise man to one in deep sorrow,*
> *"I did not come to comfort you;*
> *God only can do that;*
> *but I did come to say*
> *how deeply and tenderly I feel for you in your affliction."*[16]

SOCIALIZATION AND ALZHEIMER'S

"Socialization is important for all of us," according to the writers at anthemmemorycare.com.

But for those experiencing a form of dementia, such as Alzheimer's, it takes on an even more critical role.

Put within the context of an individual experiencing a dementia, socialization provides a controlled, yet varied climate of both human and environmental interaction. Some are intended to spark the senses, such as experiencing a new location, or smelling fresh flowers in a garden. Others may involve exposure to new faces in the form of other adults, younger people, or even animals. All are important to provide memory impaired individuals with a sense of connectedness.

As the Alzheimer's Association on alz.org points out: "Socialization proves to enhance the lives of those with Alzheimer's disease or related dementia and their care partners. We've known for some time that being social is an essential part of one's brain health with healthy diet and exercise."[17]

The article goes on to suggest four reasons why experts encourage consistent socialization for individuals with dementia (the comments are mine):

- *Gain a greater sense of inclusiveness and belonging.* Even though Bob didn't seem to miss interacting with friends, he was so much happier when he was with caring people. I could see his joy, and often he would say that he couldn't believe how nice these people were.

- *Improve brain health.* To date, there is no cure for Alzheimer's disease. From my personal experience, however, Bob seemed brighter and more alert when he spent even a short period of time with another person. Interacting on his level, feeling that he was engaging in conversation, using more words so he wouldn't forget them—all added to his overall engagement with the world outside Alzheimer's confusion.

- *Strengthen the connection to time and place.* Having some kind of routine seemed to brighten Bob's days, even though he could no longer anticipate what was on the schedule. He enjoyed a short walk each day after breakfast. Sitting down to "read" the junk mail (which he happily thought were personal letters to him) or counting the cars that passed by our house while we ate lunch kept Bob engaged and happy. Our son used to honk his horn each time he passed our home. When I told him how much his dad loved that, our son told all his friends to honk when they passed our home. Bob was thrilled to think so many friends thought of him. The simplest of things often add comfort to the childlike life of an Alzheimer's loved one (for a season, at least).

- *Enhance and maintain focus.* Bob didn't do well when there were too many activities scheduled during the day. I found that one or two opportunities were just right. If we were going to do something in the evening, it had to be early evening. One night, we went to a paint party with a friend. I was nervous about how Bob would interact: Would he even understand what he was there for? Bob sat between us for protection and security. I spoke to the instructor before the class began and explained Bob's situation. Bob's painting looked nothing like the painting we were supposed to copy, but the instructor marveled at it nonetheless, asking him to explain it (which he did) and holding it up for the other participants to see. Bob's eyes twinkled, and he grinned from ear to ear. That evening truly enhanced his life, and he was able to maintain his focus throughout. And that painting was proudly displayed on a variety of walls in our family room for all to see.[18]

Because emotions and weariness seemed to engulf me, I truly welcomed the assistance and partnership of our helpers. However, I couldn't shake the feeling that I was intruding on their lives with my needs. They all seemed happy to be with Bob, and Bob seemed happy to be with them, so why did I feel guilty? I was forever thanking them, fretting about the weather, and worrying about Bob's changing moods. They were always concocting great plans for small adventures, adjusting to time changes, and pouring love and joy into a man who was lost in his own mind.

As I look back on those years when others cared for me by caring for Bob, I think of how each of them was an answer to my prayers. But, even to this day, some of them share with me how grateful they were to have helped in a way that they could. I didn't need to feel guilty!

Don't be afraid to accept assistance. Don't feel guilty. Even amid your sadness and your prayers, you may be the answer to someone else's prayers.

GRATITUDE

There were so many learning curves for me as Bob and I walked through Alzheimer's: addressing the inability to plan for the future, the exhaustion, the sadness over the loss of dreams, the ambiguous grief, and the acceptance that I could not do this journey alone, just to name a few. I am sure these are all too familiar to each caregiver. It does take a village—family and friends—to do caregiving well. As I look back over those years of Team Bob, I am so grateful for those who came alongside us, bringing joy to Bob's heart and peace to mine.

Close to the first anniversary of Bob's death, our family invited Team Bob to a local restaurant. We called it a "Gratitude Lunch," in which we celebrated the team, expressed how grateful we were to each of them, and enjoyed a meal together. Each person received a take-home favor—an ice-cream scoop and some yummy chocolate. Two of Bob's favorite things!

Traveling Light

Alzheimer's disease isolates and discourages both the patient and the caregiver. Allow family, friends, and burden bearers to accompany you.

A Prayer to Guide You

Lord, during this time of sadness, You see right through my attempts to be strong. You see that I am broken and in great need of Your compassion. You ease the pain that rises up within me. I am no longer lonely, because I feel the power of Your presence, and Your unconditional love transforms my sorrow into blessing. Amen.

HOPE LYDA, *Prayers to Soothe Your Soul*

CHAPTER 9

TWO ROADS DIVERGE

*Sometimes there is no right or wrong. Maybe sometimes
God's just waiting to see what choice we make and then
He's gonna hold our hand and guide us down that path.*

CORIE CLARK, corieclark.com

IT WAS A BEAUTIFUL August morning. The azure sky contrasted with the golden sun and seemed to have chased any
clouds from sight. After a few days of hot, humid weather,
the day dawned with low humidity and comfortable
breezes. Perfect! Bob was in a wonderful mood. It seemed
his personality had returned, his smile was huge, and he
was content. All was well with his world. *His* world!

We had just finished breakfast: Cheerios and tea, Bob's
favorite. Sitting on our deck overlooking our backyard,
admiring the lush trees, watching our family of cardinals

pecking away at the bird feeder—what could be more idyl-lic? Our son would be over in a while to take us to lunch. We were meeting up with his friend, who managed a new hotel in our area.

The harsh reality, though, was that I hadn't slept a wink the night before, and my eyes were burning from exhaus-tion and anxiety. Oh, I put on a happy face, but inside, my nerves were shot. The truth of this day was that we were indeed going to have lunch with someone our son knew, and he did manage a facility in our area. However, for Bob, this would be a one-way trip. Following lunch, we would leave, and Bob would begin living at a memory-care facility.

This was the worst day of my life.

THE GIFT THAT KEEPS ON GIVING

When a family member starts to suffer from dementia or Alzheimer's—with time the illness progresses, making it difficult for the family members to deal with the patient. The first emotion that follows right after helplessness is GUILT![19]

Guilt was exactly what I was feeling. So many questions tugged at my heart. Could I have done things differently? Should I have had more patience? Why had I failed in my role as a caregiver? To this day, I have to remind myself that I made many visits to many places, gathered information from many professionals, sought spiritual guidance, and in the end, did what I thought was best for Bob.

If you find yourself in this particular place on your journey—choosing a memory-care unit or professional, full-time home care—know that either decision is heartbreaking. I wish I could tell you that you will feel great after you decide which route to take. Truly, there is a sense of helplessness, because it feels more and more like the situation is spinning out of control.

The night before we took Bob, I found myself looking at the starry sky. I smiled at those little flecks of light brightening the night sky. I thought, *Yes, even in this dark-decision night, there is a guiding light.* As painful as the decision was, I held hope in a trustworthy God and believed that He would guide with His lingering light. He did that for me, and He will do it for you.

The adult day-care center was a wonderful blessing for our family. Mom was still working, and this gave her peace of mind that Dad was safe, had some mental stimulation, and was cared for. As Dad's mobility and incontinence changed, we had to look for a memory-care facility.
—Hannah

It had become apparent over the past several months that Bob's care was becoming more than I, and even his wonderful caregivers, could handle. As the messages from Bob's brain stopped reaching other parts of his body, his bathroom issues radically increased, while his cognitive abilities sharply decreased. Sleep often eluded him, and when it did, all sorts of surprises awaited me in the morning. The first moments of Mother's Day greeted me with a garbage disposal filled with nails and screws—which I successfully retrieved by hand—and also incredible fear. That plumber on speed dial was getting more and more calls from me. Most of the time, all I had to say was "Hi, it's Cynthia." And his response was "I'm on my way." Clogged drains and toilets were becoming a constant part of our weekly schedule. To this day, I still don't know what they were clogged with—the plumber used to say, with a sympathetic smile, that I didn't need to know.

LAST THINGS

But this night was going to be the last night I would sleep next to my husband. We had slept side by side, often in each other's arms, through forty-eight years' worth of nights. Sometimes those nights were shared with little ones who had had a nightmare and wanted the comfort of Daddy's (always Daddy's) strong arms to scare away the monster. Sometimes those nights were shared by a sad teenager propped on the side of our bed (Daddy's side), talking through the sadness of a broken relationship. Sometimes those nights were shared by a grown-up child trying to figure out the big questions of life that only Daddy could answer. And sometimes a grandchild or two would join us for a while in that bed of forty-eight years. Now, those nights were forever over. We had been together on this journey for so many years—even this journey through Alzheimer's disease—but now, this cruel disease would separate us.

> *Two roads diverged in a yellow wood,*
> *And sorry I could not travel both . . .*
> ROBERT FROST, *"The Road Not Taken"*

I have always loved the image Robert Frost creates in these two lines. It was just how I felt that day—standing at a fork in the road, knowing that I had made a decision and praying that I had made the right one. But in the moment, I didn't want to take either road. I wished that we could go back to our free-from-Alzheimer's life. Sadly, I knew that could never be.

I kept checking the clocks. They must have all broken, because the numbers (and the hands of our old-fashioned clocks) seemed to move like sludge in a New England winter. Did I want the time to speed up or slow down? Did I just want it to be over, or could I savor these last moments together in our home? And why was my heart racing and my head pounding?

I seemed to fixate on all these "last" things and times. Oh, why didn't I appreciate them more BA (before Alzheimer's)? How I wished I could have a redo on so many things. And where were those memories hiding? I couldn't remember anything beyond these past few hours.

LIFE IN SLOW MOTION

Soon, my son arrived, and we began our slow journey to lunch. "Dad, let's take a walk around the block," Carl suggested. *Last time*, I thought. Off they went, Bob chattering away, Carl listening and smiling, yet aching deep inside. Father and son took the route Bob loved, the route we walked every day, and as always, Bob said hello to everyone they passed along the way.

Then it was time. We got into the car and drove to

lunch. Bob was greeted by our son's "friend" and given a tour of the "hotel." In the dining room, they had prepared Bob's favorite food: grilled cheese (cut into small pieces because of his inability to figure out how to eat a sandwich), grapes, chips, and soda. Bob continued chattering, encouraging the staff about the wonderful job they were doing in the restaurant. He ate everything on his plate. My plate remained untouched.

Bob's room was ready and waiting, thanks to several friends who had helped me set up everything a few days earlier. His favorite pictures were on the walls, and his name was on the door. Soon, one of the staff members asked if Bob would like to go with her to see the gardens— of course he would. "Do you mind that I leave?" he asked me. "Maybe I can help her," he assured me. And with that, we were gone: he, out to the gardens; Carl and I, out the front door.

SHARED PAIN

As I was writing the details of that day, my son texted me and asked if I remembered that moment when we stood on the other side of the door—that locked front door. He reminded me that I had hugged him and asked if I was a bad person. I said I remembered that he had cried. There we were, a son reeling from a real-life shock to the system, and his mom, Bob's wife, frozen in the reality of what had just happened. Time stood still for those moments before we slowly walked to the car and drove home in silence.

Was this how Hannah felt when she left her son Samuel

at the temple? When she walked home without him, entered her home now quiet of toddler sounds, and set out the dishes for dinner minus one? She wanted the best for her son, she had prayed over this decision, and she was sure (at least she hoped) the priest would take good care of him.

Hannah prayed to the LORD, weeping bitterly. And she made a vow, saying, "LORD Almighty, if you will only look on your servant's misery and remember me, and not forget your servant but give her a son, then I will give him to the LORD for all the days of his life . . ."

Eli answered, "Go in peace, and may the God of Israel grant you what you have asked of him."

She said, "May your servant find favor in your eyes." Then she went her way and ate something, and her face was no longer downcast. . . .

So in the course of time Hannah became pregnant and gave birth to a son. She named him Samuel, saying, "Because I asked the LORD for him." . . .

She said to her husband, "After the boy is weaned, I will take him and present him before the LORD, and he will live there always." . . .

After he was weaned, she took the boy with her, young as he was . . . and brought him to the house of the LORD at Shiloh. . . . They brought the boy

We had funds available to pay for excellent care in a private facility. I can't imagine how much harder this journey would have been with financial woes on top of everything else. My heart goes out to families who struggle in this area.

—TERRY

to Eli, and she said to him, ". . . I am the woman who stood here beside you praying to the LORD. I prayed for this child, and the LORD has granted me what I asked of him. So now I give him to the LORD . . ."

I SAMUEL 1:10-11, 17-18, 20-22, 24-28

I thought, *Yes, I know how Hannah felt.*

When we arrived home, I asked my son to drop me off, because I needed some alone time. The house was very still, seemingly asleep. I wandered through the rooms, running my hand over the striped chair where, on many mornings, Bob had sat, enjoying breakfast as he watched the cars drive by on their way to work or school drop-offs. I peered out windows to an empty lawn where Bob had spent so much time trimming his beloved shrubs. I opened the freezer and smiled as I saw a lid resting beside an ice-cream container—aah, Bob, you had one last scoop of your favorite food before you left home earlier today. And I sat on our bed—much too big for just one person.

A NEW CHAPTER

Yet knowing how way leads on to way,
I doubted if I should ever come back.

ROBERT FROST, *"The Road Not Taken"*

This was it. Life would never be the same. As "way leads on to way," there would be one less dish at the table, one less burger on the grill, one less seat belt to click, and only one person to control the remote. Which side of the bed should I sleep on? Who would shovel the snow from the sidewalk? Would I ever really laugh again? Bob and I were now living separately, yet we had vowed "until death do us part." My mind and heart were about to explode. *Breathe, Cynthia!*

So I sat in that striped chair, Bible in my lap, and began looking through pages where I had underlined certain verses. This is how the Lord spoke to my heart:

> In you, Lord my God,
>   I put my trust.
>
> I trust in you. . . .
>
> Show me your ways, Lord,
>   teach me your paths.
> Guide me in your truth and teach me,
>   for you are God my Savior,
>   and my hope is in you all day
>   long.

PSALM 25:1-2, 4-5

This is what the Lord says:

> "Stand at the crossroads and look;
>   ask for the ancient paths,
> ask where the good way is, and walk in it,
>   and you will find rest for your souls."

JEREMIAH 6:16

Those ancient paths again. The path of faith. *Will I trust in Him? Is He my hope? Will I find rest for my soul?* I asked myself. I rested my head on the back of that striped chair, pondering these questions, and I fell asleep.

I don't know how long I slept, but I do remember waking with a refreshing sense of peace. *Yes, He is my hope. I will put my trust in Him, and I will find rest for my soul.* Was it easy? No. But it was a choice, a decision I had to make for whatever days lay ahead. Placing a loved one in a memory-care facility is one of the hardest decisions to make. Each story, each journey, is different.

That first night, I received a phone call telling me Bob had a hard time falling asleep, but he was now sleeping, and I shouldn't come yet. "Give him a few days to adjust," the facility director and on-duty nurse told me. So I spent those few days at our son's summer home, joyfully distracted by the grandchildren and the scenery and deeply appreciative of the care Bob was getting. All was well, or so it seemed. Nightly phone calls assured me of him adjusting, having a good appetite, and enjoying several ice-cream treats daily.

On the fifth day, I visited Bob for the first time. What a joy to see him! He was glad to see me. He showed me his room, and we sat outside in the garden area. This went on for a few weeks. Then I began to observe increasing agitation and confusion, major mood swings, and a continual request to "take me home." Just as he had done with his home office, he packed up all his belongings. They sat in boxes all over his room, and he was ready to go home.

Then, one night, the phone call came . . .

Traveling Light

Decisions will get more and more challenging. Understand that there are no clear-cut answers, no right or wrong choices. Do what you can to prepare well for your journey, trust God to continually guide you, and keep moving forward.

A Prayer to Guide You

O Lord,

I give you my worries and concerns and I ask for your guidance. You see it all, the outer circumstances, the inner turmoil. I know that you understand my life, that sometimes my heart weighs heavy with trouble. Right now I lay all these things before you. I breathe in, safe in the knowledge that I am held by grace. I breathe out, knowing that I am held secure in your arms. And I wait on you. For you are all truth, you are overflowing love, you are a beacon of hope and a fortress of faith.

Lord, I choose to be attentive to your voice.
May I be alert to your Spirit's guiding
as I journey onwards with you.

I love you, Father. Amen.

A PRAYER FOR STRENGTH AND GUIDANCE
www.lords-prayer-words.com

CHAPTER 10

ARRIVING AT
THE DESTINATION

A journey of a thousand miles began with one step.

LAO TZU

BOB SPENT HIS DAYS at the memory-care center, and I spent
my days as a woman with a confused identity. I was not
a single woman, yet I lived alone. I was not a divorced
woman, yet my husband lived elsewhere. I was not a
widow; I visited my husband several times a week. Who
was I?

I couldn't ask my husband, because he knew me only as
a nice person who was kind to him. He had no recollection
that I was his wife, that we shared forty-plus years together,
had three children and five grandchildren. I was the only
one who remembered our shared life, the only one who
held the memories of those many years. So, who was I?

Identity is a funny thing. The way we think of ourselves, how we define ourselves, the story we tell ourselves about who we are, all of that comes together to create our identity. And yet we don't always have a conscious awareness of our identity or even a loss of identity. It often exists in the background, like the soundtrack of a film. We aren't consciously aware of it until something changes.[20]

Bob made a few friends at his new home. He ate meals with his new friend, Tony, and he responded well to the staff and continually encouraged them. He enjoyed being outside in the courtyard, did not enjoy crafts class, and had no interest in the current-events discussion group. (I have often wondered why a current-events discussion group was offered at a memory-care facility. Bob would quickly tell you that the year was 1983 or sometimes 1955.)

And so life, as altered as it was, continued. It became obvious that to keep Bob in the facility, I would have to sell our home. I walked through the rooms speckled with photos, familiar paintings, keepsakes—each with its own particular memory—but it seemed like I was just a visitor. We had lived there for forty years, yet it didn't seem like a home anymore, more like a big house with someone else's furniture and belongings.

Our son's friend was a Realtor, and she agreed to handle the sale. The task was overwhelming; if you've ever moved, you know. Our things had to be removed, so everything went into the garage. And the house was transformed with all the props that good stagers provide.

In another ring of the circus of my life, Bob was deteriorating rapidly. Late one night, the phone rang, and I heard: "You must come to the facility immediately. Bob has become aggressive and combative." My gentle and loving husband? They must have called the wrong number. Surely, they were talking about someone else's husband. In shock, I called my son to tell him where I was going. "Not alone, Mom. I'll be right there."

This was the moment our lives took a wretched turn. As I sit and write about that night, my stomach churns as deep sadness weaves its way, once again, through every fiber of my being.

This disease is so heinous because it robs its victims of the ability to understand, to think, to monitor their own basic bodily functions. Tears still flow when I miss him—not the man with Alzheimer's, but the man who was once vibrant, strong, and always knew his mind.

—JOAN

A PERFECT STORM

Bob was admitted to the geriatric psychiatric unit at a wonderful hospital. As the doctor explained, the disease was causing erosion to his frontal lobe—"the editor of the brain," he explained, "controlling behavior, outbursts, and aggression." But he assured me that they would come up with the correct cocktail of drugs so Bob could return to the memory-care facility in about ten days.

The days turned to weeks. The medical team tried one cocktail after another. All of them failed. Because of his violent behavior, Bob had to be heavily medicated. "Only temporarily," the medical staff assured me.

Our journey of a thousand miles continued, step by step. The perfect storm had descended on me: Our home was on the market, I was now living with my son's family, and Bob's life hung in the balance. The storm was raging, and the immediate was all I could deal with: Bob's rapidly declining condition was the only thing I could focus on.

Each day brought more bad news. I would visit Bob, sit at a table with him, and watch my once strong, confident husband being fed by the medical staff or running his hands in circles on the table. There was no communication from him, just an acknowledgment that he heard me—I have no idea if he knew what I was saying. It was incredibly hard for our grown children to see their dad in this condition. We made the difficult decision to shield the grandchildren and let them remember their BobBob as he was before the hospital.

One night, Carl sent a video of his teary-eyed eight-year-old son asking if his aunt (our daughter who works in the pharmaceutical industry) could make a special potion that would cure BobBob because he loved and missed him. That broke our hearts! But no potion was to be found, and soon, blood clots started making an appearance.

BITTERNESS

During these dark days, I found myself thinking about Naomi. To escape a famine in Bethlehem, Naomi left with her husband and two sons. Her husband died. Later, her two sons married Moabite women. Ten years later, both of her sons died.

When Naomi heard in Moab that the LORD had come to the aid of his people by providing food for them, she and her daughters-in-law prepared to return home from there. . . .

When they arrived in Bethlehem, the whole town was stirred because of them, and the women exclaimed, "Can this be Naomi?"

"Don't call me Naomi," she told them. "Call me Mara, because the Almighty has made my life very bitter. I went away full, but the LORD has brought me back empty."

RUTH 1:6, 19-21

"Oh Lord," I prayed, "I don't want to become bitter. I don't believe You have afflicted me. I believe with all my heart that You have been with me through this lengthy journey and You will bring me out somehow, in Your time. Keep my focus not on what I am losing, but on all that I have."

I thought of Job, who lost so much but put a hand over his mouth (Job 40:4) when he realized his position before a sovereign God. I thought of Mary, who pondered all things in her heart, and those things gave her courage through the pain of watching her son die. I thought of Peter, who denied Jesus three times but was lovingly restored when Jesus asked, "Do you love Me?" And I thought of all the saints who "did not receive the things promised; they only saw them and welcomed them from a distance" (Hebrews 11:13). I remembered what I told the doctor on the day of Bob's diagnosis: "I'm going to live on the other side of eternity."

Bob's eternity seemed to be growing huge on the horizon.

There were treatment decisions to be made, questions I
never thought I would have to answer, sadness so deep that
it carved a hole in my heart. There were no
words to describe how I felt. My concern
for our children and grandchildren was
overwhelming, and I found myself pondering so many things in my heart as a lifetime
of memories cascaded in and through my
spirit. I kept placing a hand over my mouth
as I recalled the many times God had lovingly intervened in our lives.

*Frankly, I am
ready for my dad
to be whole again.
I will miss him
terribly . . . I can
go hug him now
and see him smile.
This is not how
he would have
wanted to spend
his final years.
I am comforted
in the knowledge
that he will be
fully restored the
moment he takes
his last earthly
breath.*

—HOPE
(Hope's dad died
while I was writing
this chapter.)

I had plenty of time to think because
nothing else mattered, but clear thinking seemed to elude me. Sitting with Bob
gave me comfort, even though he said
nothing. We were two people who had
looked forward to a future together, yet
now I faced that future alone. Two people
who laughed together, prayed together,
and loved together, yet neither of us was
laughing, and only one of us was praying.
But I do believe that somehow, we were
both loving each other and God. I have to
believe in the psalmist's words:

> Yea, though I walk through the valley of the shadow of
>   death,
> I will fear no evil;
> For You are with me.
>
> PSALM 23:4, NKJV

Bob was not alone, and neither was I. God was accompanying each of us, about to be separated by eternity: Bob journeying to see his Savior, and I remaining here. And God was present for each of us in just the way we needed:

[God said,] "Never will I leave you;
    never will I forsake you."
HEBREWS 13:5

God was with us in the hospital day room and through those lonely dark nights. Because

The LORD will fight for you; you need only to be still.
EXODUS 14:14

And that was all I could do—be still.

One Sunday afternoon, my daughter and I were sitting with Bob as he made circles with his hands on the table. His speech was garbled, and it was difficult to understand the few words he would speak. But suddenly, he looked at us and said, clearly and confidently, "God is taking care of me. I just want to go home."

My daughter and I looked at each other. If it weren't for the fact that we were together, we probably wouldn't have believed the clarity in the words we had just heard. Bob just wanted to go *home*. Not his previous requests in the memory-care facility of "take me home."

Bob looked at me and said, once again clearly and confidently, "You're a pretty girl." Then back to the circles on the table, but this time with my arms around him and tears of gratitude streaming from my eyes.

Those were the last words Bob spoke. And I will treasure them as a gift straight from heaven.

Life kind of moved in slow motion after that. He was now confined to his bed. One special night, a dear friend came in to pray with us and anoint Bob with oil. This was the leg of the journey Bob would take alone. Our family sat by his bedside, watching as the final effects of Alzheimer's ravaged his body.

Mom has been home with Jesus for almost three years. I still cling to the fact that she is home and no longer broken; she is whole again. The hardest thing for me is that she is not here for us to love on and to watch her grandchildren grow. She always wanted to be a grandmother.

—KELLY

I was determined that his room would be a holy space: conversation was quiet; one of us was either holding Bob's hand or rubbing his arm. Morphine dulled his pain, yet our pain was raw.

We sat with him as he passed through the torment of life's final stages: grasping up for something to his right, thrashing about, occasionally trying to jump out of the bed. I came to believe the words of an oncologist friend: "Dying is hard work."

Early one Tuesday morning in October 2016, Bob stopped thrashing, became very calm, opened his eyes, and took one last look at me, then at our son and daughter. He exhaled his last earthly breath and then, I am convinced, inhaled celestial air.

The room was quiet and still, tears silently flowing as we processed what had just taken place. It was a holy moment.

In an instant, Bob was *home*. My heart and emotions fluctuated between grief and relief. The world stood still. Nothing else mattered.

Death for a believer is not the end of life. Actually, it's just the beginning. It's the transition when our faith becomes sight, and real life begins. We can look forward with hope because we are going home![21]

THIS SIDE OF ETERNITY

The reality of Bob's death engulfed me like a tsunami. I tried to stay afloat as all the practical details swirled around me, shouting for my attention: plan his memorial service, close on the sale of our home (which took place the morning of Bob's memorial service) . . . and breathe!

Bob's memorial service was a tribute to Bob's life and gave glory to God. Throughout the service, I sat transfixed by God's goodness and faithfulness. I was in awe of His care for both of us through these difficult years and His guidance when I didn't know the way. We celebrated Bob's life during the memorial service and with an ice-cream sundae bar at the luncheon that followed. We thought it was fitting.

A few weeks following Bob's memorial service, I drove down our old street, thinking I'd look at our home, now sold and due to be renovated. There it was: *not* our house, but a huge hole in the ground. The house was gone.

Gone! I had to pull over and turn off the ignition because I was sobbing so heavily. Bob was gone, and now the home where we lived and raised our children, the home that welcomed our precious grandchildren to play in the backyard with their beloved BobBob—was all gone. The tears flowed, and I begged God to help me make sense out of these losses. As I looked back at the vacant lot, I couldn't help but think of all the sadness and loss that life contains on this side of eternity. *Yes*, I thought, *I'm glad I decided to live on the other side of eternity, putting my confidence not in earthly things but in heavenly ones.* Scripture says, "Set your minds on things above, not on earthly things" (Colossians 3:2).

While there was, and is, plenty of pain on this side, it's important that caregivers aren't too hard on themselves. Don't expect to have no tears, to have a constant smile on your face, to have it all together all the time. In a time of grief, be real with yourself, be human, and be still.

Traveling Light

All loss is painful. Multiple losses are heartbreaking. Begin disciplining yourself with the practice of setting your mind and heart on eternal things.

A Prayer to Guide You

Lord, at the moment nothing seems to be able to
help the loss I feel.
My heart is broken and my spirit mourns.
All I know is that Your grace
is sufficient. This day, this hour
Moment by moment
I choose to lean on You,
For when I am at my weakest
Your strength is strongest.
I pour out my grief to You
And praise You that on one glorious day
When all suffering is extinguished
and love has conquered
We shall walk together again.

A MODERN PRAYER FOR COMFORT IN GRIEF
www.lords-prayer-words.com

CHAPTER 11

REFLECTIONS

God allows us to experience the low points of life in order
to teach us lessons that we could learn in no other way.

STANLEY LINDQUIST, *True Genius*

OUR JOURNEY TOGETHER is over. Bob is safely at his destination. I'm on a new journey now.

Looking back, I see I've gained insights, learned valuable lessons, and enriched my life. Our trip contained some very painful moments . . . and some very sweet ones.

I hope it has strengthened my faith. The prospect of growing old alone (although I am so grateful I have family and friends) does not excite me. But if God has brought me through this trip, He can and will take care of me the rest of the way as my solo journey now continues, on another uncertain road. I must look ahead, but every good driving instructor will tell you that an occasional glance in the rear-view mirror is important for safe travel.

James reminds us in the opening chapter of his epistle:

Consider it pure joy, my brothers and sisters, whenever you face trials of many kinds, because you know that the testing of your faith produces perseverance. Let perseverance finish its work so that you may be mature and complete, not lacking anything.

JAMES 1:2-4

While I don't believe that God tests us, I do believe that He allows certain life experiences so we will grow and our faith will be strengthened. There were many times during those thirty-four months as Bob's caregiver when I wanted to have a conversation with God and ask just what it was that I was supposed to learn. "Give me a book, Lord," I would say, "and I'll read it and learn all the lessons necessary for a whole and complete life." But a book was not part of the process. Real learning happens only from real experience.

Many years earlier, a friend had shared this insight with me from the book of Genesis: Joseph did not learn any lessons during his time languishing in a pit (Genesis 37:23-28). Yet God used the pit to form insights and convictions that would shape Joseph and an entire nation (Genesis 50:20). No lessons were learned while Alzheimer's came close and became personal. But I clung to my belief that God would not waste anything, that He was still sovereign, and that one day, I would emerge from this valley—how and when, I didn't know.

Each day of those thirty-four months took perseverance, total reliance on God, and trust. Yet these truths had to be relearned each day. Now that I have emerged a bit from my valley, I have done some hard thinking. Looking back has helped me look forward.

The following are some of the lessons I learned and am still learning. Perhaps not every lesson applies to you, but I pray that there are some truths here that will strengthen you for your ongoing journey.

PEOPLE GRIEVE DIFFERENTLY

It has been almost two years since Bob went home. I still weep, but not from sadness. The tears come when something stirs a sweet memory: "Bob would have loved that joke," or "Our grandson said that just like BobBob would have." When one of our children or grandchildren reaches a milestone, I think how proud Bob would have been. I view these tears not as a weakness but as a tribute to my full-of-fun, kind, and encouraging husband.

ACCEPT REALITY

The harsh reality of Alzheimer's disease is that the diagnosis is a shock and the prognosis is a death sentence. At this point, there is no cure, and medications provide only minimal and temporary help.

I had learned the medical statistics, so I was not going to spend time trying to find a doctor who would offer some wonderful, miracle cure. Nor would I listen to well-meaning folks who told me about some amazing new diet that reverses memory loss. I would just smile and say that the concept was interesting, but I knew the grim facts. I'd remember a greeting card I bought just for me:

SORRY,
THE LIFESTYLE
YOU ORDERED
IS
CURRENTLY
OUT OF STOCK

Once, when speaking at a neuroscience symposium and sharing about life as a caregiver, I was asked if I had read the book *Still Alice*. I responded no, and I explained that I believed Bob was not "still Bob." I had to learn to embrace who he was at that moment and in all the moments to come.

Where did all my wisdom come from? Certainly not from me. I was still stumbling and learning. But the Bible says that "if any of you lacks wisdom, you should ask God, who gives generously to all without finding fault, and it will be given to you" (James 1:5). Accepting reality helped me to live in the moment and trust Him for the future.

I learned that lesson daily, because I had no idea what tomorrow would bring.

Imagining what things are like for my mom in heaven, without pain and with a restored mind, often tears me apart. Her death was a blessing, yet it was still hard. The final parting left a hole.
—DONNA

LIFE IS SHORT—BE KIND

It was one of Bob's favorite statements: From the time
I met him, whenever I was hurt by or upset about someone, he would always remind me, "Cynthia, life is short. Be
kind." Bob lived those words. I don't know of anyone who
would say that Bob ever uttered a sharp word to them. He
spoke truth but with kindness.

When he would go for a walk with one of his Team Bob
friends, they would return and tell me how Bob stopped to
talk to everyone, always offering a word of encouragement.
The police officer walking through the center of town, the
woman at Dunkin' Donuts who loved to serve him, the
distant neighbor working in his yard—all received kind
words of encouragement from a man who had no idea who
he was talking to but considered each a friend in need of a
kind word.

Toward the end of Bob's earthly journey, when he was
heavily medicated and had to be fed, the hospital staff
would continue to tell me (sometimes with tears in their
eyes) that each time his meal arrived and each time a staff
member finished feeding him, Bob's response was always
"Thank you!"

Every morning, I ask the Lord to give me an opportunity to be a blessing, to extend kindness to someone.
A lesson learned from a man who practiced it daily.

IT'S THE DISEASE TALKING

Very early in my journey, my friend and colleague Dana
shared these vital words with me—words that sustained me

throughout our uncertain road: "It's the disease talking." Dana was ahead of me in her mother's Alzheimer's journey, so she spoke with validity and was a voice of experience. Four simple words, yet they were life-giving. As Alzheimer's robbed Bob of his personality, he sometimes spoke words that were hurtful, sad, and even downright mean. Yes, even kind people can say hurtful things. "It's the disease talking" became the filter through which I received these words, and that filter protected my heart. I attributed the words to the disease and not to Bob's heart toward me.

Of course, there were times when I felt like I was at the end of my rope. What should I do? I had to acknowledge my very human frustration. At these challenging times, I would turn away for a second or two and scream silently at the wall. As strange as it seems, I then found myself more able to deal with the situation at hand.

I shared my "scream at the wall" discovery with a friend a bit behind me in her uncertain road of Alzheimer's. She called me a few days later and said, "It works! Thank you so much."

I find great comfort in the words of Darlene, a dear friend who is a caregiver to Alzheimer's folks: "Alzheimer's cannot steal our souls. It can hold the mind in its sharp grip, but never the soul." It was, and always is, the disease talking.

BUILD HOLY HABITS

A habit is an acquired mode of behavior that has become largely, if not completely, involuntary. Bob seemed to learn the secret of holy-habit living early in life, and until the disease completely took over his mind, he lived those habits: encouragement, contentment, and trust.

I was always amazed at Bob's attitude. Though confused so much of the time, though dependent on me for every decision, though unable to conduct any meaningful conversation, though unable to read and eventually write, Bob trusted God.

Intentionally build holy habits into your life to sustain you through the valleys when they come. A lesson learned from one who lived it.

HAVE "THE CONVERSATION"

When Bob's condition worsened and his care intensified, the hospital staff had lists of questions for me. As sad as this season was, I felt incredibly well prepared to respond to their questions about Bob's palliative care. My preparation was not based on my medical wisdom; rather, I was speaking Bob's words and wishes. Over the years, sometimes during those long walks, we had discussed our thoughts and wishes about end-of-life matters. We were not sick or old; we were just talking. Our thoughts flowed freely because the time was so far away and, as far as we were concerned, that time might not come. But talk we did. Sometimes we would joke about what we wanted. But we never joked about what we didn't want.

The time did come—much sooner than I would have liked. But when the doctors began by saying, "This is a really difficult question," it really wasn't. I am so deeply grateful that Bob and I talked freely and often; it made the difficult questions a bit easier. Not less sad, but easier. My encouragement to all is to have those conversations while you are young, while you are healthy. The time will come, and the questions will be asked. Will you be prepared?

KEEP SHORT ACCOUNTS

Like all married couples, Bob and I argued. I knew that the Bible says we are not to let the sun go down on our anger (Ephesians 4:26). I used to joke with Bob, saying, "Well, the sun is shining somewhere in the world!"

One day, many years ago, Bob and I visited some very dear friends while we were vacationing in Florida. This couple had their share of challenges—the brilliant husband had a serious medical incident causing him to spend twenty years like a little child, being lovingly cared for by his wife. We loved spending time with them, loved seeing her strong character and his sweet nature. One day, while three of us were engaged in a very deep conversation, Mark kept interrupting. His wife, Karen, lovingly looked at him and said, "Not now, Mark." He replied, "Okay, sweet Karen."

That simple interchange marked our lives from that day on. On the way home, Bob suggested that one of us, during an argument, should respond, "Okay, sweet Bob," or "Okay, sweet Cynthia." And we did for a long time.

When Alzheimer's robbed Bob of the ability to reason and remember, it also gave him the ability to keep short accounts, precisely because he couldn't reason or remember. If he didn't remember what he said, or why I was upset, what good did it do for *me* to remember?

"Bear with each other and forgive one another if any of you has a grievance against someone. Forgive as the Lord forgave you" (Colossians 3:13). A freeing lesson learned in the furnace of Alzheimer's disease.

KEEP YOUR EYES ON THE ROAD

I had to keep focused. The only social circle I could maintain was of people who made time for us, for me. There were friends (some I hardly knew) who would just stop by the house and thereby help me believe that we hadn't been forgotten.

One friend, Rebecca, would pull into the driveway, ring the doorbell, and hand me two cups of coffee from our local coffee shop. She'd give me a hug and then go on her way to a meeting or a class. She's a busy lady, but she took time to let me know she remembered us. I will be forever grateful.

There were those who acknowledged that our situation was hard and often awful and extended grace, not instruction. And then there were those who passed judgment, telling me that I wasn't handling things the way I should. They had better ideas. Well, they didn't live in my world, and I just couldn't deal with it—I had to maintain focus and keep my eyes on the road. For those fractured relationships, I grieve, but I do not carry guilt.

"Whether you turn to the right or to the left, your ears will hear a voice behind you, saying, 'This is the way; walk in it'" (Isaiah 30:21). A lesson learned through loss, on many levels.

LIVE AN OPENHANDED LIFE

Many years ago, I learned of a study that had determined that we open and close our hands about twenty-five million times in our lives. So, I did the math and had it checked by Bob, my engineer husband: If the average life span is seventy years (at least, that is what the Bible tells us!—see Psalm 90:10) and there are 365 days per year, then we open and close our hands just under a thousand times a day. I learned, as a caregiver, that I had to hold things very loosely.

I am a fixer by nature, so I tried finding creative ways to help Paul continue functioning as normally as possible by adapting his tasks, making lists, leaving Post-it reminders, and working with him. But when these fixes failed, I felt I had failed as well.

—SARAH

When things broke, or things got lost, I learned not to spend too much time worrying about them. Eventually, they would show up, or I would forget about them. And when I did, God could then fill my hands with His things. My prayers for a long time had been three simple words: "God, help me." I read an article (I gave up reading books because they were too long and I had too little time) that challenged me to change those three words to three different words: "Make this count." I began to refer to this as my "openhanded prayer."

That Mother's Day morning when I woke to find the garbage disposal filled with nails, screws, and bolts, I prayed, "Make this count." After turning off the disposal, I stuck my hand in and removed the items a few at a time.

If my hand was clenched around too many items, I couldn't have removed my fist. Truly a lesson in openhanded living.

As Alzheimer's stole Bob's mind, I watched him loosen his grip on many things, yet he tightened his grip on God. Many times each day, he would say, "God is taking care of me." Was his response directed at anything in particular? No, just a statement of truth he believed in his heart. A lesson learned as I watched a man walk through a dark valley, releasing his grip on things that held no value.

INTENTIONALLY PURSUE GRATITUDE

During our long walks together over the years, Bob and I would talk about our kids (and eventually our grandkids), discuss our lives and our plans, work through hectic schedules, solve our problems (and, often, the world's problems). I loved those walks and always returned refreshed.

As Bob's illness increased its grip, our walks became shorter and our conversations became simpler. Oh, how I missed those stimulating conversations. We kept walking, though, sometimes just to the corner of our street and back. The shorter walk was okay with Bob—he was content. I, on the other hand, was gaining weight from lack of exercise.

When Bob entered the memory-care facility and I was faced with doing life alone, walking wasn't something I looked forward to. After a few days of resistance, however, I started out on the old route. As I stood at the end of our driveway, wanting so much to turn around, I decided to thank God as I walked. Hard as it was to get started,

I began to walk and talk. I talked with God about everything I was thankful for: a loving family, a safe place for Bob, the beautiful summer flowers, our church, my faith, a car, the sunshine—you name it, I thanked God for it.

That first day, what I thought was going to be such a hard walk became a holy experience. I literally walked past our driveway because I was so caught up in the things for which I was thankful. God became my walking companion. When gratitude seemed challenging, I thanked Him for who He is. I thanked God alphabetically: Almighty, Beautiful Creator, my Deliverer, my Eternal Father, a Good and Gracious God . . . all the way to X, Y, and Z. Gratitude became a holy habit. It made me aware of God's presence and His faithfulness, it drew to my mind the many ways God had intervened during the past months, and it refreshed my mind and heart.

Following Bob's death, I thanked God each time I drove by a nursing home, grateful we didn't have to make the torturous decision to place Bob in one. I continue, even now, intentionally pursuing gratitude. Why? Because gratitude is a game changer, a heart changer, a life changer.

There are times when I feel myself starting to grumble. Yet gratitude rushes in like a minesweeper, and my attitude changes. A lesson learned at a time when the world wanted me to believe that I had nothing to be thankful for.

LEARN THE POWER OF PRESENCE

My first day at church after a three-month absence, I wasn't ready to face many people, and I was concerned about too many people talking to me. What would I say? What would they ask? How would I feel?

I sat in the balcony with a friend. It seemed safe enough. The benediction was given, and I walked out, eyes down, emotionally exhausted and just wanting to get to my car. But I felt a tap on my shoulder. When I turned, a man was standing there, his arms opened wide. I knew him: I had served on teams with him, and he was a casual friend. There were no words; he just wrapped me in a big bear hug, then let me go. Such a warm and comforting moment!

The power of presence—it was life-giving. Too often, we worry about saying the right thing to someone who is hurting. Words aren't necessary. Presence is!

I have pondered this concept, and as I reflect on those who spent time with me, I see that the most helpful were the ones who said very little. Sometimes, they just sat with me and let me talk. They didn't give answers, solutions, or formulas. They just listened. They invited me into a holy place—a place where I could be myself, a place where I didn't have to say anything, a place where I knew I was understood. They pointed me to God just by their presence. "Be still, and know that I am God" (Psalm 46:10) was the gift they gave me.

All too often, people stay away because they don't think they have anything of value to offer. This is more painful than anyone can imagine. There were many who helped me, though: Team Bob folks who took Bob for walks or for lunch, who spent time with him; those who occasionally brought a meal; those who sent notes to remind me they hadn't forgotten us; and those who sat with me on the "mourning bench," knowing there were no answers, no quick fixes.

> There is a ministry of "presence." The fact that you are there with the one who is suffering can often help more than any words you say.[22]

Give someone the gift of yourself. Stay for a short time. Bring some flowers from your garden, a cookie from the bakery or your own kitchen, but most importantly, bring yourself. A lesson learned by the example of those who gave me themselves, their time, their love, and their presence.

DO YOUR JOB

I don't know much about football, but since I live in New England, I am a die-hard Patriots fan. Coach Bill Belichick is known for constantly reminding his team: "Do your job!" I interpret that to mean stay the course, do what you are called to do, and don't give up.

This is similar to the caregiver's journey through Alzheimer's. All the lessons above hinge on focus: Stay the course, keep on keeping on. God will supply what you need. And then, when the journey is over, we—you and I—still have a job to do.

Throughout Scripture, God asks, "What is in your hand?" Moses had a stick, and he used it to part the Red Sea. David had a slingshot and five smooth stones, and he used them to slay Goliath. The little boy had five loaves and two fish, and Jesus took them and fed over five thousand people. And he asks us today, "What is in your hand?" What will you do with the lessons you learned and the growth you experienced in the Alzheimer's valley?

For me, writing this book is my gift to the Alzheimer's world. I pray that through reading about my experience, others will be encouraged and strengthened.

Jenifer's mother, Linda, died of Alzheimer's disease in 2012. Jenifer and her mom loved to go out to eat, but as the disease took over Linda's mind, eating out was too much for her. Jenifer now hosts "Linda's Lunches" at her restaurant, The Red Raven, in honor of her mother. Caregivers and loved ones with Alzheimer's come together for lunch on the first Saturday of each month. There they enjoy fellowship and socialization.

Jenifer is also the founder of "Purple Table Reservations." When you call the restaurant and request a Purple Table Reservation, the host knows you are coming with an Alzheimer's patient. Upon arrival, you will be seated in a quiet area of the restaurant, away from the TV and near the restroom. Your server, trained to care for an Alzheimer's individual, will carefully explain the menu and give attentive service. Jenifer is "doing her job" with what has been placed in her hand.

What about you? When this portion of your journey is complete, what will be in your hand? What will you do with the gifts He has given you? A lesson learned by trusting God for the beginning, middle, and end.

IT'S ALL ABOUT LOVE

We usually think of love as a two-way street, but as Bob retreated deeper into his own world, he was unable to show his love. I would hug him, but he wouldn't hug me back. He no longer spoke the words of love that had been such a natural part of our relationship. Love now felt like a one-way street. Yet, showing Bob my love brought me joy. Love is not about what I get, it's about what I am willing to give.

To my friends caring for a loved one who may not be as pleasant as you think Bob was, please understand that he certainly had his moments. I learned early on that living in his "Disney World" was far easier than trying to correct him when he became agitated or downright fresh. If he believed that green was red and up was down, that was the final answer. I had nothing to prove to Bob except that I loved him and he was safe with me.

This is what it's all about. As I reflect on my journey with Bob through the valley of Alzheimer's disease, I know that God walked with me (with us) through it all. Yet He didn't force me to acknowledge His presence and guidance, to lean on Him for every breath I took and every decision I made, to trust Him through it all. He didn't force me to love Him during those dark, difficult, and seemingly impossible seasons. Nevertheless, my love for Him brought—brings—Him joy.

God is the only One who knew the twists and turns of our uncertain road. And He is the only One who can now heal the sadness of Bob's absence. The implications of this truth are new and remarkable, and they give me hope. A lesson I learned by giving my love with no expectation of anything in return.

What was the totality of the lessons I learned during that season? That I didn't have to make plans, that I didn't have to know what the next year would bring, that I didn't have to cling to the dreams of what I had thought life would be but rather cling to the truth that God knew, and that was sufficient. This perspective brought me a new freedom.

My journey had begun with a single step. And as I ponder, even today, my identity, my life, and my journey, I am reminded that "God is taking care of me" and I'm "a pretty girl."

Traveling Light

God doesn't waste anything. Lessons will come at the end of the journey.

A Prayer to Guide You

Dear Lord, I thank You for Your constant companionship, for walking with me through the valley of the shadow of death, and for bringing me out into Your light. Thank You for blessing me with the freedom to trust You, to lean on You, and to receive Your loving care each moment. When I felt I couldn't go on a minute longer, You carried me until I received strength again. When I wept, You reminded me that "You keep track of all my sorrows. You have collected all my tears in your bottle. You have recorded each one in your book" (Psalm 56:8, NLT). There truly is no one like You, and I love You with all my heart.

CYNTHIA FANTASIA

EPILOGUE

It wasn't until recently that some members of Team Bob—these precious caregivers—thanked *me* for the opportunity they had to spend a part of Bob's journey with him.

At first, I would take Bob to church on Wednesday mornings to help do repairs. Afterward, we would go for a long walk—we did lots of walking. Bob would tell me about Lexington and the great job the town government had done, about our church and the founders, and we usually talked about his growing up in Quincy. When helping out at Grace Chapel got too much for Bob, we started having lunch dates on Wednesday.

In the process, I learned a lot about Bob. The Alzheimer's stripped away any pretenses. What I saw was a man who really loved people. He would talk with anyone, and he was sure he knew almost everyone walking down the street in Lexington. He could carry on a great conversation, and people were happy to talk with him. I remember a conversation with a neighbor who was working in his yard when we were walking back to Bob's home. Bob complimented him on the great job he was doing and how beautiful his yard was.

In Bob, I saw a man who loved the church and loved the Lord. I remember his ongoing concern because he wanted everyone to know Jesus. He was always the encourager. When I visited him at the memory-care facility, he always thanked the workers for the great job they were doing. It was great to see the smiles on their faces from Bob's encouraging words.

Bill

It was so freeing to be with Bob. Everyone he met was his friend. No qualifications needed. He loved telling people they were doing a good job. Each time we were together, he would bring into our conversation: "I've had a good life."

When it was too cold to walk outside, and when walking was too much for Bob, we would go to my house, enjoy a cup of tea and a cookie, and sit by my fireplace. One day, I asked Bob, "What is it about a fireplace that makes us want to keep watching?"

Bob responded, "It takes all of your worries away. I don't have any worries." And then, "I've had a good life."

Bob could talk for long periods of time with many repetitions and random thoughts. I developed a greater power of concentration to be attentive and to respond or maybe ask a question. He loved to be asked a question and to give advice. He had such a nature of desiring to be helpful.

On our fall walks, Bob would always choose a few red leaves to collect. To my eyes, those red leaves were torn, worn, ragged, and very imperfect. I was reminded that Jesus loves the torn, ragged, worn, imperfect us. Bob loved people just as they were.

Some of the lessons I learned from my time with Bob:

I've learned to listen even when I can't understand. I've learned to ask the right question to make someone feel valued for their opinion or answer.

I've learned to make eye contact and keep my mind focused when conversation is limited.

I've learned to be drawn in by sweetness, gentleness, and love.

I've learned to choose, love, and applaud the imperfect red leaf.

Beth

Bob was always so kind and happy to talk about his family. I shared with him about my family, and it was a blessing for me to spend time with him. God is good, and I think we enjoyed each other's company.

Dieke

Bob taught me how to relax and enjoy nature by sitting in the backyard on a beautiful summer day, enjoying the birds that would visit. Bob never seemed to be in a bad mood when I was with him. He always had a funny story to tell.

Bob didn't value napping. He was always on the go. When eating a snack, he was always generous in offering some of his food. When we went to Dunkin' Donuts, he would talk to everyone. He always mentioned what a hard worker Danita was and how nice she was to all her customers.

Bob enjoyed reminiscing about his childhood and his appreciation of his family. This gave me an appreciation for my own family roots.

Time spent with Bob was God's way of telling me to chill out and enjoy the simpler things in life.

Eileen

When I first agreed to spend time with Bob, I didn't know him well. As Bob declined, I remember thinking that it must be overwhelming for Cynthia to be the sole caregiver 24/7, that she could really use a hand, and that I was available to offer that hand. I felt a tug on my heart to be the servant and encourager that God calls us to be.

I quickly began to look forward to the walks all those months. Bob always had a smile on his face, which lifted my spirits. As we walked and talked, I used to think that here is a man obviously with so much intellect, experience, and accomplishments, yet the memories and thoughts were being robbed from him. It saddened me on one hand; however, what remained was a simple, very sweet, thoughtful man. His conversation always sought out the best in people and places and circumstances. I marveled at how he saw everything with a rosy sheen. I observed beauty in his sight.

This caused me to think more about my outlook and how I frequently looked at the coarser side of life. My time with Bob allowed me to adjust to a slower pace, to relax, to be unhurried in the short time that we were together, with nothing on my mind but where a conversation might take us. It was a time to break from a hectic life and take in the simpler beauty around us. Bob opened my eyes to this.

I also felt immensely blessed in blessing Bob and Cynthia. There's great joy and contentment in knowing that you are needed and helping someone else. Isn't that what we're here for, to walk alongside each other on our earthly journey? It may only be a fleeting moment, a lifelong friendship, or anything in between, but we are here together to love one another.

Lisa

These people didn't consider it a burden to be with Bob—they looked at their time with him as a blessing. I couldn't believe it. What a gift they gave us, how my heart soared, and how humbled and grateful I was to know that even in his illness, Bob was a blessing to others.

These were my traveling companions. People who shared their life and time with Bob. My heartfelt thanks to each of these companions, who showed such practical love to Bob and me.

A Prayer to Guide You

May God's love and truth bring
clarity and purpose to your life.
May His strength steady your steps.
May His compassion open your eyes
and may His conviction
make your heart beat strong.
May His Kingdom come and His will
be done in and through you.
Rest in His truth.

SUSIE LARSON, *Blessings for the Evening*

A NOTE TO CHURCHES

MOST OF MY PROFESSIONAL CAREER was in full-time ministry. For almost twenty-five years, I served as pastor of women at Grace Chapel in Lexington, Massachusetts. Throughout those many years, I have seen how the power of God and the people of God make a difference. People have invited me into their deep hurts and their delightful joys. Exploring the Word of God has illuminated the way for many groping in the dark. And when the Word prompts people to care for others, a beautiful thing happens. But I have also seen the human side of church people who, over time, move away from those dealing with a lengthy illness.

I have always believed that the local church is the hope of the world. Hope is what a hurting world hungers for.

It's what those struggling with and caring for someone with Alzheimer's disease need. Hope is oxygen for the soul. In the pages of this book, I have shared my hurting soul, which was empty at times. I have also shared how many came alongside me (and Bob), offering care and hope. And yet, this type of response is not common in most church families.

> "The churches have failed their people," says ethicist and expert on aging, Stephen Sapp. "Specifically in the area of support for persons with Alzheimer's and their caregivers."[23]

While there is not yet a cure for Alzheimer's disease, and death is always the prognosis, the church can and should lead the way to offer care and support during the Alzheimer's season.

> The estimated number of Americans with Alzheimer's disease and other dementias has risen to 5.7 million, from 5.5 million in 2017, according to a report released today by the Alzheimer's Association.
>
> That's an increase of roughly 3.6 percent and largely reflects the aging of the boomer generation.
>
> By 2025, the 2018 Alzheimer's Disease Facts and Figures report projects, 7.1 million Americans aged 65 and older will have Alzheimer's, and by 2050, some 13.8 million.[24]

These numbers speak for themselves: Alzheimer's is "among us," and every church will be affected. The church is in a unique position to reach out to Alzheimer's families with the love of Christ and a helping hand. The seven suggestions that follow were birthed out of my personal experience of "It would be so wonderful if . . ." Feel free to adapt these ideas to the size, needs, and resources of your church.

1. *Spiritual-Based Support Groups.* I did not attend any support groups while I cared for Bob. I would have loved a group that had a spiritual component, so members could encourage one another to trust in the Lord and His faithfulness. Financially, it would have been challenging to find care for Bob while I was at a support group. Churches could offer a combination: a support group for caregivers and, in another area of the church, a program for the loved ones with Alzheimer's. A few volunteers to help with some easy puzzles, music, and simple art work, along with an approved snack, would give the caregivers a brief respite and their loved ones some socialization.

2. *Sunday School Class.* A class based on simple Bible stories using pictures and music would speak volumes to people struggling with Alzheimer's disease. Memories of Bible stories learned as a child, simple Bible verses, old hymns, and an opportunity to share would pour value into each person. And caregivers would benefit by seeing their loved ones recall the truths of Scripture.

3. *Life Stories.* Bob loved to look through old photographs. Even if he didn't remember names, he would

often share stories (some fictional) about the photos. A great activity for a team of volunteers would be to visit someone with Alzheimer's to document a "life story" through photos and memories. It would be an activity with long-lasting significance as the disease increases and the memories become more distant.

4. *Time, Talent, Treasure.* The entire church family can be involved in pouring value into a person with Alzheimer's. Watch for ways the person can be made to feel valuable. If a table needs to be moved, ask the person to help you move it. If books need to be carried to another room, ask the person for assistance. The smallest of tasks, the simplest of chores can offer a feeling of normality and acceptance to one who feels useless and isolated otherwise.

5. *Memory Café.* Started in the Netherlands in the 1990s, Memory Cafés are gaining popularity in many senior centers. It's a place for those with Alzheimer's and their caregivers to get together for an hour or so, enjoying simple refreshments and conversation with others. A church could offer the same to its families: Volunteers could make coffee and cookies, and family members could drop in for a comfortable time together—not worrying about what people around them are thinking.

6. *Education.* A church could create a brochure providing facts about Alzheimer's and listing ways members can show care and offer help.

7. *A Place to Ask.* Many senior centers have volunteers who are available to answer questions about finances, health insurance, taxes, repairs, and other problems. A church could ask members who are retired professionals to volunteer their time and experience to help caregivers address the myriad of details they must now face alone. Many times, an individual is perfectly capable of sorting through these kinds of challenges . . . until he or she becomes a caregiver. Then, it's all too much! The volunteer can point out when the caregiver needs a professional for particular topics. Just knowing there is a place that offers some guidance is a life-giving gift.

Dr. John Bisagno, retired pastor of First Baptist Church in Houston, Texas, has said, "I have most often seen that, when the people of God are presented with the facts, they do the right thing." As Alzheimer's disease increasingly affects our population, I pray that the people of God will indeed do the right thing. I pray that the "least of these," whose memories are fading and whose families are devastated, will find they do not walk alone through their valley. May they, and their caregivers, be accompanied by burden bearers who share the love of Christ and give the practical help necessary.

NOTES

1 Kim Maryniak, "The Needs of Patients and Families with Alzheimer's and Other Dementias," https://www.rn.com/clinical-insights/alzheimer -dementia/, accessed January 10, 2019.

2 Ken Bishop, "Out Living," http://kenbishop.md/outliving/out-living, accessed January 10, 2019.

3 None of the men I asked were willing to share, unfortunately. I can't speak to their reasons for not responding, but men do tend to be more taciturn than women, and many men default to an "I can do this" independence that might incline them not to share their struggles as caregivers. The deep loneliness that can attend to such an approach to caregiving is an increasing area of concern in the medical community.

4 Lewis Carroll, *Alice's Adventures in Wonderland* (CreateSpace, 2018), 32.

5 "Caregiver Stress," https://www.alz.org/help-support/caregiving/caregiver -health/caregiver-stress, accessed January 10, 2019.

6 "2018 Alzheimer's Facts and Figures," https://www.alz.org/alzheimers -dementia/facts-figures, accessed January 10, 2019.

7 Henri Nouwen, "Enough Light for the Next Step," https://henrinouwen .org/meditation/enough-light-for-the-next-step/, accessed January 10, 2019.

8 Rend Collective, "Weep with Me," from the album *Good News* (Sparrow, 2018).

9 Paula Spencer Scott, "Alzheimer Caregiving Essentials," https://www .caring.com/articles/alzheimers-caregiving-and-parents, accessed January 10, 2019.

10 Ibid.

11 Esther Heerema, "How Does Dementia Affect Long-Term Memory?" July 21, 2018, https://www.verywellhealth.com/long-term-memory-and -alzheimers-98562, accessed January 10, 2019.

12 "Ambiguous Grief: Grieving Someone Who Is Still Alive," https:// whatsyourgrief.com/ambiguous-grief-grieving-someone-who-is-still-alive/, accessed January 10, 2019.

13 Ravi Zacharias, *Jesus Among Other Gods* (Nashville: W Publishing Group, 2002), 85.

14 Paul Borthwick, "10 Ways for Avoiding 'Shriveled Soul Syndrome,'" July 14, 2017, http://www.paulborthwick.com/10-ways-for-avoiding-shriveled -soul-syndrome/, accessed January 10, 2019. Adapted with permission.

15 Skye Jethani, *Singing at Midnight* (self-published by the author, 2016), 11.

16 Tryon Edwards, *The New Dictionary of Thoughts* (Amazon Digital Services, 2015).

17 "Socialization for Dementia Care: 5 Reasons Why It's So Important," August 14, 2016, https://www.anthemmemorycare.com/blog/socialization -for-dementia-care-5-reasons-why-it-s-so-important, accessed January 10, 2019.

18 Ibid.

19 "Making the Decision to Move Your Loved One to a Memory Care Assisted Living Residence," Life's Journey Senior Living, November 21, 2017, https://www.lifesjourneymc.com/2017/11/21/making-the-decision/, accessed January 10, 2019.

20 "I Don't Know Who I Am Anymore: Grief and Loss of Identity," January 30, 2018, https://whatsyourgrief.com/dont-know-anymore-grief-loss -identity/, accessed January 10, 2019.

21 Anne Graham Lotz, "Looking Forward with Hope," July 10, 2014, https:// billygraham.org/decision-magazine/july-august-2014/looking-forward -with-hope/, accessed January 10, 2019.

22 Sandy Lynam Clough, *Prayers to Soothe Your Soul* (Eugene, OR: Harvest House, 2010).

23 Jade C. Angelica, "Alzheimer's Caring: How Faith Communities Can Serve People with Dementia and Their Families," December 14, 2015, https:// www.huffingtonpost.com/jade-c-angelica/alzheimers-caring-how -fai_b_8790336.html, accessed January 10, 2019.

24 Beth Baker, "Americans with Alzheimer's Now Number 5.7 Million," March 25, 2018, https://www.forbes.com/sites/nextavenue/2018/03/25 /americans-with-alzheimers-now-number-5-7-million/#445ba84b4b62, accessed January 10, 2019.

RECOMMENDED RESOURCES

The Fellowship of the Suffering: How Hardship Shapes Us for Ministry and Mission, by Paul Borthwick and Dave Ripper. Downers Grove, IL: InterVarsity Press, 2018. A valuable guide to and through the how (not the why) of the dark and disappointing days.

God in the Dark: 31 Devotions to Let the Light Back In, by Sarah Van Diest. Colorado Springs: NavPress, 2018. A devotional using the Psalms as a guide and a reminder that He is always with us.

Hidden Manna for the Caregiver, by Charles W. Shepson. Morris Publishing, 1995. This book of brief devotionals provided much comfort as I began my journey as a caregiver. Shepson, a caregiver to his wife, spoke truth to my sadness and encouraged my heart.

Little Pieces of Light: Darkness and Personal Growth, by Joyce Rupp. New York: Paulist Press, 1994. A little book offering encouragement to value the darkness as a place to know God deeper.

A Promise Kept: The Story of an Unforgettable Love, by Robertson McQuilkin. Wheaton, IL: Tyndale, 1998. A tender yet direct memoir of a man who cared for his wife through her struggle with Alzheimer's disease.

When Bob no longer was able to stay focused, these two devotionals, each entry brief, were very encouraging for me and very comforting for Bob.

- *Blessings for the Morning: Prayerful Encouragement to Begin Your Day*, by Susie Larson. Bloomington, MN: Bethany House, 2014.

- *Blessings for the Evening: Finding Peace in God's Presence*, by Susie Larson. Bloomington, MN: Bethany House, 2013.

The following are websites that I found helpful (there are others as well). Each one will lead you to more links that are also helpful. Reading stories on these websites gave me insight into how others were handling their experience.

- Alzheimer's Association: www.alz.org

- National Institute on Aging: www.nia.nih.gov/alzheimers

- "The Forgetting: A Portrait of Alzheimer's": www.pbs.org /theforgetting

- Caring.com: www.caring.com

- Best Alzheimer's Products: www.best-alzheimers-products.com

ACKNOWLEDGMENTS

THIS BOOK IS A TEAM EFFORT. From the very beginning, as Bob and I journeyed through Alzheimer's, Team Bob formed, kept us company, and offered support through the valleys and the plateaus. Since Bob went home and the words to this book appeared on reams of paper, Team Cynthia has kept me company and offered support in so many ways.

It all began five days following Bob's memorial service. I had registered for a conference earlier in the summer, but I felt it was just too soon to attend anything. I was raw and exhausted. But my friends Rachel and Cindy convinced me to come with them, promising never to leave my side. I knew they meant it. I knew I could trust them. And they even told me that if I became too overwhelmed, one of them would drive me home. It was that day I had a conversation with Don Pape, an acquaintance from many years before. He offered me his condolences for Bob and then suggested I write a book about our journey. It was the furthest thing from my mind, and I didn't take his suggestion seriously. But his encouragement touched a chord in my heart, and I took that first step. I was a reluctant writer, but Don, you believed in me, and so I forged on. Your consistent encouragement—a few phone calls, emails just when I needed them, and the ever-present knowledge that you believed I could do this—spurred me on. Thank you for believing in me when I didn't believe in myself. I am forever grateful.

There were many friends who prayed for me and this book, and for you I am so grateful. Three women formed a team of prayer warriors and faithfully prayed for me every day. Darlene Gibson, Carolyn Miele, and Beth Scott: When I thought I couldn't peel back another memory, another pain, your prayers lifted me above the fog, helping me see the view clearly. Thank you for your prayers, your friendship, your encouragement. You have prayed me to the finish line, and I am forever grateful.

Linda Doll: What can I say? From the very beginning, you offered me wisdom, allowed me to brainstorm my muddled thoughts with you, were patient when my words just didn't come easily, cried with me when I shared tender thoughts, and kept telling me that this was going to be a really good book. You have become one of my dearest friends, and I am forever grateful.

David Zimmerman, editor extraordinaire! As an oldest child with a type A personality, I was so nervous about an editor reading my material. I worried about the red marks and the bad grade I might get. But you have great ideas, you "got" what I was struggling to say and suggested a better way to say it, you offered outstanding suggestions about the structure of this tale, and you gave me incredible encouragement. I learned so much from you. I am forever grateful.

To my children and grandchildren: You have kept me going. I see Bob in each of you, hear his voice in the words you speak, and love to remember him through your memories. Life does go on, a little sadder and very different, but we are the keeper of Bob memories, and I am grateful that you love to share them. I am forever grateful for your love, your support, and your laughter.

To Bob: This is your story. Thank you for forty-eight years of love and shared life. Thank you for your courage and your love for God and me. As your light grew dim, His light lingered, and that one day in October 2016, it shone extra bright and guided you home. I am forever grateful.

And to Jesus, without whom I could never have walked the Alzheimer's journey: You are a faithful, strong, and loving Savior. I am the humble recipient of the abundant life You came to give. I am forever grateful.

CREDITS

REFLECTIONS from "Team Bob" and "Traveling Companions" are reproduced with permission. The names of the "Traveling Companions" have been changed.

Prayers from *The Book of Common Prayer* (chapters one and six), the rights in which are vested in the Crown, are reproduced by permission of the Crown's patentee, Cambridge University Press.

The prayer by Tracie Miles (chapter two) is copyright © 2016 by Tracie Miles (traciemiles.com) and originally appeared at https://proverbs31.org/read/devotions/full -post/2016/11/28/godly-friends-godly-wisdom. Used by permission. All rights reserved.

The prayers by Hope Lyda (chapters four and eight) are taken from *Prayers to Soothe Your Soul*, copyright © 2010 by Harvest House Publishers, Eugene, Oregon 97408, www.harvesthousepublishers.com. Used by permission.

"Daily Prayer—One Moment at a Time" (chapter five), from the Missionary Society of St. Columban website, www.columban.org, is reprinted with permission.

THE NAVIGATORS® STORY

THANK YOU for picking up this NavPress book! I hope it has been a blessing to you.

NavPress is a ministry of The Navigators. The Navigators began in the 1930s, when a young California lumberyard worker named Dawson Trotman was impacted by basic discipleship principles and felt called to teach those principles to others. He saw this mission as an echo of 2 Timothy 2:2: "And the things you have heard me say in the presence of many witnesses entrust to reliable people who will also be qualified to teach others" (NIV).

In 1933, Trotman and his friends began discipling members of the US Navy. By the end of World War II, thousands of men on ships and bases around the world were learning the principles of spiritual multiplication by the intentional, person-to-person teaching of God's Word.

After World War II, The Navigators expanded its relational ministry to include college campuses; local churches; the Glen Eyrie Conference Center and Eagle Lake Camps in Colorado Springs, Colorado; and neighborhood and citywide initiatives across the country and around the world.

Today, with more than 2,600 US staff members—and local ministries in more than 100 countries—The Navigators continues the transformational process of making disciples who make more disciples, advancing the Kingdom of God in a world that desperately needs the hope and salvation of Jesus Christ and the encouragement to grow deeper in relationship with Him.

NAVPRESS was created in 1975 to advance the calling of The Navigators by bringing biblically rooted and culturally relevant products to people who want to know and love Christ more deeply. In January 2014, NavPress entered an alliance with Tyndale House Publishers to strengthen and better position our rich content for the future. Through *THE MESSAGE* Bible and other resources, NavPress seeks to bring positive spiritual movement to people's lives.

If you're interested in learning more or becoming involved with The Navigators, go to www.navigators.org. For more discipleship content from The Navigators and NavPress authors, visit www.thedisciplemaker.org. May God bless you in your walk with Him!

Sincerely,

DON PAPE
VP/PUBLISHER, NAVPRESS

www.navpress.com

CP1308